The Sex Education
Controversy

Lexington Books Politics of Education Series
Frederick M. Wirt, Editor

Michael W. Kirst, Ed., *State, School, and Politics: Research Directions*

Joel S. Berke, Michael W. Kirst, *Federal Aid to Education: Who Benefits? Who Governs?*

Al J. Smith, Anthony Downs, M. Leanne Lachman, *Achieving Effective Desegregation*

Kern Alexander, K. Forbis Jordan, *Constitutional Reform of School Finance*

George R. LaNoue, Bruce L.R. Smith, *The Politics of School Decentralization*

David J. Kirby, T. Robert Harris, Robert L. Crain, Christine H. Rossell, *Political Strategies in Northern School Desegregation*

Philip K. Piele, John Stuart Hall, *Budgets, Bonds, and Ballots: Voting Behavior in School Financial Elections*

John C. Hogan, *The Schools, the Courts, and the Public Interest*

Jerome T. Murphy, *State Education Agencies and Discretionary Funds*

Howard Hamilton, Sylvan Cohen, *Policy-making by Plebiscite*

Daniel J. Sullivan, *Public Aid to Nonpublic Schools*

James Hottois, Neal A. Milner, *The Sex Education Controversy*

The Sex Education Controversy

A Study of Politics, Education, and Morality

James Hottois
University of San Diego

Neal A. Milner
University of Hawaii

Lexington Books
D.C. Heath and Company
Lexington, Massachusetts
Toronto   London

Library of Congress Cataloging in Publication Data

Hottois, James.
  The sex education controversy.

  Bibliography: p.
  Includes index.
  1. Sex instruction—United States. 2. Family life education. I. Milner,
Neal, joint author. II. Title. [DNLM: 1. Conflict (Psychology). 2. Sex
education. HQ57.3 H834s]
  HQ57.5.A3H68   375.6139'5   72-469
  ISBN 0-669-83634-6

Published simultaneously in Canada.

Printed in the United States of America.

International Standard Book Number: 0-669-83634-6

Library of Congress Catalog Card Number: 72-469

To
Jo-Elle, Gregory, Robert, Joanna

Contents

List of Figures   xi

List of Tables   xiii

Preface   xv

Introduction   xvii

Chapter 1   The Politico-Moral Principles of Sex
Education in the Schools   1

Moral Values and Sex Education   3
The School and Politico-Moral Conflict   5
Policy Implications   8
Moral Conflict and Political Conflict   10

Chapter 2   Sex Education: The Orientation Issue   13

The Psychological View   14
The Political Conflict-Social Control
Approach   18

Chapter 3   Community Educational Policy Making   21

Educational Innovation   21
Community Educational Policy Making   25
Policy-Making Techniques   27
Local Educational Policy Making: Some
Hypotheses   32

Chapter 4   Professionalization and Innovation   35

The Generation of Need   35
The Content of the Professional Literature   38

School Superintendent Professionalization   42
General Innovativeness   44
Conclusion   46

Chapter 5   **Sex Education Policy Making and the Failure of the Opposition**   47

Opposition Failure   47
Content Alteration   50
Opposition and Counterinfluence   51
Conclusion: Conflict Mitigation, Opposition
    Failure and the Availability of Resources   59

Chapter 6   **Innovativeness Reconsidered**   63

The Structure and Process of Innovation   64
Innovation and Discontent Management   66
Conclusion   70

Chapter 7   **Sex Education in Anaheim and Statetown: Two Case Studies**   73

Anaheim   73
Statetown   78
Comparison of the Anaheim and Statetown
    Cases   86
Summary   90

Chapter 8   **Sex Education and Social Control: Some Broader Issues in the Politics of Education**   93

The Perspective Restated   93
Summary   94
Analogies: Sex Education and the Courts   95
The Provocative Nature of the Perspective:
    Authority and Participation   100

Appendixes 103

    Appendix A: The Data 105
    Appendix B: The Questionnaire 111

Notes 125

Index 135

About the Authors 137

List of Figures

5-1   Patterns of Consideration of Family
                Life/Sex Education   48

List of Tables

1-1	National Attitudes Toward Sex Education in the Schools 1943-65	12
4-1	Interest in Sex Education in the Education Profession and the Public and the Year it was First Considered by School Districts	37
4-2	Sources of Opposition and Support for Family Life/Sex Education	41
4-3	Stand of Superintendent, School Board, and Citizens During First Consideration of Family Life/Sex Education	42
4-4	Superintendent Professionalism and Consideration of Sex Education	44
4-5	Comparison of Relative Speeds of Innovation	46
5-1	Result of Reconsideration and Level of Opposition	50
5-2	Frequency of Topics Taught in Sex Education Programs	51
5-3	School Superintendent Attitudes about Participation in Educational Policy Making	53
5-4	Level of Opposition and Policy-Making Mechanisms used in SEP Considerations	54
5-5	Policy-Making Mechanisms and Level of Opposition—First Consideration	55
5-6	Committees of Public Meetings and Opposition Level—Both Considerations Combined	56
5-7	Policy-Making Mechanisms and SEP Comprehensiveness	58

5-8   Committees, Public Meetings, and SEP
        Comprehensiveness—Both Considerations
        Combined   58

5-9   Rank-Order Correlations Between Opposition
        and SEP Comprehensiveness   59

6-1   SEP Comprehensiveness Controlling for
        District Innovativeness and Level of
        Opposition   68

6-2   SEP Comprehensiveness Controlling for
        District Innovativeness and the Use of
        Unilateral Policy Making   69

A-1   Geographical Distribution of Responses   108

A-2   Responding and Nonresponding Districts in
        the Deep South   109

A-3   Responding and Nonresponding Districts
        Outside the Deep South   109

A-4   Percent of Questionnaires Returned Compared
        to Percent of Responding Districts with
        Comprehensive SEPs   110

Preface

This book is the product of many different changes in attitude, perspective, and emphasis. The introduction elaborates upon these changes; here we would like to thank those who helped bring them about.

In gathering the data, we had to intrude upon the time of school superintendents, very busy people indeed. We thank them for filling out yet another questionnaire. In order to get a better grasp of the specifics of sex education programs, we interviewed a number of school officials and teachers, especially in Statetown (see Chapter 7) and Cedar Rapids, Iowa.

"We" here refers to more than just the two authors. A group of bright and resourceful undergraduate scholars helped us at all stages of the investigation. It was Diana Onerheim, Mark Meyer, Linnet Harlen, and Beverly Schneible who maintained the project from day to day.

Many people and a variety of institutional settings gave us the opportunity to develop our perspective on sex education and educational policy making. None of these people should be held responsible for the final version of this work, but whether or not they agree with us, their contributions were invaluable. The study began with a grant from Grinnell College that allowed us to do almost all of the survey work. Neal Milner spent the 1971-72 academic year at the Center for the Study of Law and Society at the University of California, Berkeley, under the auspices of a National Science Foundation Science Faculty Fellowship. This fellowship gave him an opportunity to discuss his ideas with an extraordinary group of graduate students and faculty members from a variety of disciplines. He would like especially to thank Phillip Selznick, then director of the center, and Sheldon Messinger, then dean of the School of Criminology of the University of California, for their part in fostering this atmosphere. James Hottois spent a summer working with other political scientists at the Public Policy Research Organization, the University of Minnesota, under the auspices of the National Science Foundation. This provided him with the opportunity to reflect upon the policy process.

Many others have read all or some of our manuscript or patiently listened to our ideas. They include Ed Greenberg, Michael Shapiro, Michael Mezey, Jack Dukesberry, Karl Schumann, Stan Cohen, Bob Grey, and Ralph Rossum. David Lewis of Computer Timesharing Corporation provided valuable assistance and advice. Special thanks must go to Fred Wirt, the editor of the series in which this book appears. He was patient with our tardiness, penetrating in his comments, and gracious in his criticism. He had more to do with holding this project together than he realizes.

The manuscript, at various stages, was typed by Patti Blumer, Dorothy Perez, Shannon Moore, and Margo Davidson.

Since this book is about sex education and conflict management, it is only fitting that we dedicate it to our children.

Introduction

Every so often a seemingly minor event dominates the political agenda in completely unanticipated ways. Thus it was with the issue of sex education in the schools. Quite abruptly in the late sixties, the mass media began to discuss the rancorous conflict in some communities over the issue of sex education. One typical reacton was incredulity: "With all the war and racism, who cares that school officials want to talk about sexuality in class?" Still, sex education seemed to have all of the trappings of a major political issue. National interest groups became involved. For the proponents, the Sex Information and Education Council of the United States (SIECUS) became a leading clearing-house for information on the subject, and its membership was very active in encouraging programs. Mary Calderone, the executive director of SIECUS, was interviewed in *Playboy*, and much of that interview considered sex education. The American Medical Association and the National Education Association also took positions rather firmly supporting school sex education.

The opponents also had the support of some important national organizations. The John Birch society actively encouraged opposition to such programs and frequently attacked the proponents' goals, motives, abilities, and political ideology. Other objecting organizations familiar to students of the radical right, such as the Christian Crusade, also made vigorous and vituperative attacks on what they viewed as the sex education establishment.

Indeed, as Mary Breasted has shown in her sensitive book on the subject (the only real attempt to come to grips with some basic questions about the issue), a sex education establishment did exist. School sex education became professionalized, and the professionals held national conventions where the largest educational publishers attempted to sell the extensive new wares they had developed. On the other hand, national conventions of radical right organizations used opposition to sex education as a primary means of rallying support for a major attack upon the American educational system.[1] The members of the President's Commission on Obscenity and Pornography manifested these conflicts in microcosm.

Certain communities that had pioneered in the development of school sex education programs were suddenly forced to retrench. In Anaheim, California, the program that its administrators eagerly hoped to make the model for the entire country was crippled as a result of intense community opposition. Indeed, the events in Anaheim became the mass media's paradigm for the issue.

On the basis of this brief description, one could view the controversies over school sex education as "typical" community conflicts in which a small but intense minority of "right-wingers," supported by national interest groups, succeed in administering another defeat to the more "cosmopolitan" and more "progressive" school administrators. The previous description, in sum, stresses community conflict, the involvement of nationally oriented rather than locally oriented interest groups, and success of the opposition.

We must admit that our initial interest in school sex education was almost entirely based on this rough paradigm. Both of us were interested in theories of community conflict, and we initially chose school sex education as an issue to test and revise those theories. In short we assumed that the most analytically interesting aspect of the controversy was its clarity as a form of community conflict. But as we will show in the following chapters, our assumptions were misleading. Conflict and opposition were indeed important characteristics of the controversy, but we discovered a great deal more about the activities of educational policy-makers—and about our own values—that made us switch the emphasis of our study. Rather than stressing the intensity of conflict and the success of the opposition, this study concentrates upon the techniques that school officials used to mitigate conflict and to limit success of the opponents. Some of this change in emphasis is no doubt inherent in our methodology, which is detailed in an appendix to this book. Much of our study is based on information from approximately five hundred relatively large school districts. We did not select these districts because they had experienced conflict over sex education with Anaheim's results. Thus, not surprisingly, we found that the Anaheim type of conflict was more exceptional than the mass media led one to believe.

But much of our change in orientation was based on something more compelling than methodological techniques. Choice of research methods is of course a value choice, but we found ourselves confronting our own value position in more indirect and, for us at least, more surprising and important ways. We shall now elaborate upon these ways, not merely because we feel that social analysts' values ought to be clarified in advance, though this alone is an important reason. Nor do we offer the elaboration as a rationalization for our ambiguity and confusion, though we are most anxious to show the readers that they too, upon reflection, may find the lines of battle less clear and their values less certain.

Issues of sexual behavior involve basic value choices that cannot be ignored even by two authors who maintain extensive social distance from their subject by studying bits and pieces of material based on a national sample. We immersed ourselves directly in only two community sex education controversies. Still, we found ourselves raising questions about our values regarding tolerance, education, and community participation. This is most clearly manifested in our ambivalence toward the advocates of school sex education. Prior to our study, we both accepted the notions that sex and sexual behavior ought to be more fully divorced from guilt and that the school was one proper place to carry this out. We still strongly accept these notions in the abstract, though we are less sanguine about the schools' role, not just because of their ineffectiveness, but because there are some competing values.

Our ambivalence about these values developed because the most active proponents of school sex education either completely ignore some important issues or severely underestimate their importance. For example, we found ourselves asking: "Who should have the authority to develop sexual values and how tolerant should such authorities be of opposing values?" One usually assumes that this is the kind of question that gets asked of opponents of sex education, who are typically accused of attempting to impose their values unilaterally on a socially pluralist society. But in fairness, the question should apply to *both* sides. To what degree can or should those advocating or offering school sex education consider the views of those who are less willing to accept this pluralism? Putting it more baldly, how tolerant should promoters of school sex education programs be of people whom they find basically intolerant? It is a serious and perplexing issue, which we could not expect school policy-makers to solve. Still, their failure even to confront the question is disappointing. Generally, the proponents' answers are disappointing or nonexistent. They tend to hide behind a screen of value freedom and fail to recognize that tolerance and the encouragement of diverse viewpoints are themselves moral positions. We had previously rejected the either-or moralism of the traditional moralist, but as the study progressed, we also found ourselves rejecting the allegedly value-free perspective of the proponents.

We also found that our values toward the substance of sex education sometimes conflicted with our values about procedure. We found appealing the idea of discussing questions of human sexuality in the classroom but were somewhat disturbed by the methods that generally were used to adopt such programs. Despite our opposition to the substantive goals of school sex education's most rigorous opponents, we found ourselves concerned by the fact that they were frequently what Robert Dahl would call an "intense minority."[2] Our system of government supposedly protects such minorities from the wishes of either a "tyrannical majority" or government bureaucrats, but, of course, this protection is in fact problematical. The professionalization of policy-makers and their ability convincingly to define an issue as being within their own professional sphere of competence are techniques and processes that limit the participation of active minorities. There are obviously other limitations, but for our purposes, professionalization is the most critical. The educational policy-making process typically discourages effective mass participation, though our political values generally stress the need for broadening citizen participation in decision making. We are, of course, not the first to confront the dilemma between innovation and participation.[3] Sex education should be considered in this context because of the role it plays in increasing our ambivalence toward the issues. We found ourselves studying a situation where a process we do not generally like was used rather successfully to limit the success of a group whose political positions we did not like. Much of Chapters 3 through 7 concerns the means used by policy-makers successfully to limit the effects of opposition, and in Chapter 8 we attempt to deal with this dilemma. But, at the risk of redundancy, we ask the reader to keep these considerations in mind, not so much because we solve the problems nor even confront all the value choices explicitly or directly. Rather, it is important to do so because the deceptively frustrating issue of school sex education compels a person to rank his or her values and to confront such issues as the importance of tolerance and the primacy of participation.

Note the change in emphasis. From the brief discussion of Anaheim one gets the impression that the main question may be "How do we keep the minority from imposing its will on the majority?" Our own values and focus shifted to the degree that we feel that the phrasing of the question is misleading or, more accurately, incomplete. We think that questions involving the policy-makers' tolerance of, and empathy toward, intense minorities are equally important issues. If we seem to stress the latter too much, our best excuse is that we think that most people need this kind of reorientation because their own views make it likely that they see the issue in the more conventional way.

Our study does not focus upon the propriety of these various values, but again we hope that the reader will develop an empathy for them if for no other reason than because much conventional wisdom suggests such empathy is not important when the radical right is involved (see Chapter 2).

It is interesting to note that Mary Breasted had a similar reaction to her subjects. At the time of her study she was a reporter for the *Village Voice* in New York City with a life style that in many ways was precisely the kind that opponents would fear that their children might develop, at least partially, as a result of school sex education. Her book also starts off in a curiously introspective way, and the chronicle of her change in orientations is as fascinating as her analysis of the proponents and opponents. Like us, she never came to accept the opponents' values about sex, but she did develop a greater sympathy for the opponents' claim that educators favoring sex education in the schools failed to confront some basic questions.

In her discussion of social science's contribution to the understanding of sex education, Mary Breasted concisely states what can probably be considered the limits of our own work:

I had been banking on the hope that social science would provide the final elucidation of this odd controversy I had set out to chronicle. Social science would tell me whether sex education did, in fact, influence behavior. Social science would tell me why sex education had suddenly struck the hearts and minds of considerable numbers of parents with fear. Social science would tell me why, in Anaheim California, where 92 percent of the adults said they supported sex education, its opponents had, for the present, triumphed. . . .

It turned out, of course, that social science was not in the possession of all the answers, and those answers that it had were only fragmentary, only "instruments" for continuous speculation.[4]

Perhaps our own study can offer the basis for little more than continuous speculation. Even so, changing the *nature* of speculation is important when a controversy engenders so many predictable prejudices. To succeed in getting people to see the issue in a different light and, as a result, to speculate upon it in ways that are new to them is no mean accomplishment. We hope that our study at least does that.

The Politico-Moral Principles of Sex Education in the Schools

Conflict over sex education in the schools is important not just because of what it tells us about schools, but also because it reflects a basic difference in politico-moral values. In American society, the vitality of the Protestant ethic has declined, replaced by a set of values that is more consistent with the present economic system of corporate capitalism. This set of values is less concerned with maintaining the entrepreneurial spirit than with encouraging consumption. Instrumental and rational activity are still highly valued, but there has been an important relaxation of the Protestant prohibitions against expressiveness and hedonism. A consumption-oriented society "requires that men cease to be ascetic and self-denying and abandon many of the guilts that they experience when they express their impulses."[1] This is not to say that the new ethic encourages unfettered libertarianism. On the contrary, it stresses the need for management and control. A basic difference between it and the values related to the Protestant ethic is that the older set of values stressed the need to *deny* one's impulses rather than to *control* them.[2]

The distinction between denial and control is subtle but important. Implicit in the denial of impulse is the view that it is illegitimate to discuss sexual matters unless the discussion focuses only upon "legitimate" sexual behavior and only if it clearly states the correct moral standards. Advocates of the control ethic believe that wide-ranging sexual discussions are important because by bringing such matters into the open, an individual is best able to understand impulses and thus to control them. The denial ethic stresses the importance of maintaining a sense of guilt regarding "illegitimate" impulses, while that of control believes that the alleviation of guilt is the best means to avoid the unhealthy manifestations of sexual impulses.

The difference between the two sets of values is reflected both in views concerning the kinds of policies advocated and the kinds of institutions that implement these policies. The Protestant ethic stresses the need to continue rigid control over man's sexual behavior by avoiding much self-expression. One way of achieving this control is by denying the legitimacy of the impulses. It emphasizes the use of coercive sanctions like the criminal law to maintain such control. The newer ethic's emphasis upon the sometime contradictory ideas of impulse management and self-expression rather than self-denial is accompanied by an emphasis on the use of institutions that can best handle the need for control. Both sets of values accept the need for state action but differ significantly over its proper forms.

1

Because self-denial is such an important part of the old Protestant ethic, this position views the school as a risky institution for the inculcation of moral values. Even though the educational system has been used as a relatively effective form of management in some cases, its emphasis on the desirability of expressing oneself, of holding open and frank discussions, threatens an important aspect of already severely threatened values. The discussion itself makes the old ethic seem less legitimate. In short, to the extent that sexual standards are to be discussed, the church and the family are the more proper and more reliable communication institutions.

We shall subsequently develop these distinctions further. Here they are sketched merely to elucidate the basic components of the conflict. The previous discussion suggests that the political conflict certainly has an important moral dimension. It also suggests that these differences in moral views are important because they are related to fundamental political values involving self-restraint, tolerance, and self-expression. Finally, the discussion sensitizes us to the importance of the school in this conflict. To say that the controversy centers around the school because that is the institution the proponents of sex education choose begs the question of why it is chosen. Such a statement underestimates the significance of the school for the broader political values in conflict here.

Because sex education is related to such important value differences, the issue would seem to be subject to particularly intense and even rancorous conflict. When one's morality is threatened in such a basic way, the willingness to recognize the legitimacy of an opponents' views—a prerequisite to easy conflict resolution—is severely, if not completely, limited.[3] The issue can evolve into a conflict of basic principles, the kind that a system based on compromise cannot easily tolerate. To put the issue more specifically in terms of community processes: conflict develops when community members are affected in diverse ways by events that are perceived to be important.[4] The issue of sex education seems to have at least the potential amount of diversity and importance to lead to such conflict.

We shall elaborate the basic principles behind the conflict over sex education in the schools, not to show how conflict actually develops in various communities but rather to demonstrate the issues around which the conflict would develop if it were not mitigated in some way. Or, putting it more in terms of those who desire school sex education programs, we seek to describe the most basic, and thus the most difficult to resolve, situation these proponents might face. Though the following considers only the principles involved and not the dynamics of the conflict itself, it can and will be used as a guide to see what conflict over sex education would be like if there were no resources available in a community to limit the conflict. What follows thus may be considered an example of the principles that would set the parameters in an unmitigated conflict. It is an ideal type and thus serves as a useful source of comparison to our subsequent discussions of what really happened in school districts across the country.

Our discussion of the principles is based on an analysis of the works of the leading spokesmen on the issue of school sex education. This, of course, tends to exaggerate the degree of difference in principles. This exaggeration is rather unimportant for our purposes, because we use the information not to analyze community conflict itself but to develop an ideal type.

Moral Values and Sex Education

As noted, impulse control and impulse denial form the basic differences in the moral principles relevant to school sex education. At times, control-oriented moral principles of the proponents are obscured by the notion that the advocates of sex education in the schools favor a value-free sex education program. Occasionally their position is even described as a form of moral relativism, one that on the surface appears to stress the cultural pluralism of American society and the consequent difficulties arising from the acceptance of a single, and what the proponents of sex education would call rigid, moral position. "Whose [moral] code is to be taught in the schools of this pluralist society?" ask the authors of an influential sex education textbook. "The minute a school tries to establish a code about masturbation, for example, or premarital sex, petting and necking, dating, and other such subjects, it is placing itself in a precarious position."[5]

In fact, the dominant proponent position is not a relativistic one, because, consistent with its interest in impulse management, it establishes some guidelines for determining the morality of an act. It does not advocate the equal acceptance of all sexual behavior but only that whose consequences an individual rationally determines, optimally by means of some form of empirical research. It is a form of situation ethics, a "morality of consequences, based upon the assumption that the judgement of acts should be related to their effects."[6] This is not to say that every individual is to follow the rigors of the scientific method when deciding on the morality of a sexual act. But it does mean that individuals have an obligation to consider systematically and to try to forecast the possible consequences of their proposed acts.

The paramount concern is not with the development of a single morality but with the development of a decision-making process that helps the person make his or her own choice. Frequently called the "valuing process," its aims are to teach a form of rationality whose criteria are based on the quality and quantity of information the individual has at his disposal to make decisions. Even though it is not relativistic, this position nonetheless leans toward viewing the study of morality as an analysis of a series of different precepts of right and wrong, all of which at least must be discussed. The existence of a variety of cultural views of sex requires that the schools avoid the assumption that value systems are actually absolute.

Thus, despite assertions that their policies are value free, the proponents, though sometimes reluctantly, advocate some forms of freedom of choice and diversity. The valuing process that they advocate encourages the individual to choose from a range of alternatives. On some issues the range may be small, but it is seldom limited to a single alternative.

The opposing moral position starts with a totally different view of morality. Sexual morality is indeed a specific set of precepts of right and wrong that have been traditionally accepted by Judaeo-Christian culture. These precepts must be taught in an explicit and forthright manner. Public policy must legitimate and reinforce these traditional values of self-restraint and parental authority and not add its force to the increase in the immoral permissiveness of modern society.[7] A child must be taught about sexual morality in such a way as to *narrow* rather than to increase the range of moral alternatives open to him.[8] The proponents might also desire this narrowing, but they are not willing to limit alternatives by refusing to discuss them. The opposition view is likely to recognize certain moral precepts that must "obviously" be protected.[9] These precepts and the behavior that violates them are clearly related to self-restraint: "chastity, modesty, temperance, and self-sacrificing love," all of which are threatened by "lust, excess, adultery, incest, homosexuality, bestiality, masturbation, and fornication."[10] In this view, while the opposing moral position may not explicitly advocate any of these evils, the refusal to teach a single set of moral precepts and to develop a more clearly defined path toward sexual self-restraint clearly limits the likelihood that the correct moral choice will be made.

There are also important differences concerning the propriety of knowledge of sexual behavior. According to the view advocating control and self-expression, knowledge about diverse sexual attitudes and practices is a key to freedom from the restraints of sexual fear and repression. "Knowledge [about sex] is safer than curiosity," typically claimed one developer of a sex education program.[11] It is indeed viewed not only as safer but as fundamental to the successful living that comes through the ability to recognize and thus manage sexual impulses. Witness the goals of a leading organization is the struggle for sex education, the Sex Information and Education Council of the United States (SIECUS):

As a nonprofit, voluntary health organization, its [SIECUS's] ultimate goal is to develop values useful for individuals in determining attitudes of responsible sexuality. Through a comprehensive program of community services, public and professional education and research information . . . to establish man's sexuality as a healthy entity; to identify the special characteristics that distinguish it from, yet relate it to human reproduction, to dignify it by openness of approach; study, and scientific research designed to lead toward its understanding and its freedom from exploitation.[12]

Compare the even more explicit statement by those on the President's Commission on Pornography and Obscenity who strongly advocated sex education in the schools:

Failure to talk openly and directly about sex has several consequences. It overemphasizes sex, gives it a magical, nonnatural quality, making it more attractive and fascinating. It diverts the expression of sexual interest out of more legitimate channels, into less legitimate channels. Such failure makes teaching children and adults to be fully and functioning sexual adults a more difficult task. And it clogs legitimate channels for transmitting sexual information and forces people to use clandestine and unreliable sources.[13]

Note that, as anticipated, the proponents are also concerned lest sex be made "more attractive" and "fascinating." Still, the differences in values are important. Again the rhetoric of this position conceals a clear set of values. The position accepts the propriety of the free flow of ideas about sex because the demystification of sex is seen as a desirable goal. Tolerance and diversity may be important in their own right, but they are particularly important in achieving sexual demystification and ultimately a more rational means of sexual self-control. Only in an atmosphere that condones and encourages a tolerance toward other ideas can this process take place.

The opposing view does not accept the contention that the demystification of sex will channel curiosity into more legitimate directions. The mere discussion of certain topics without the accompanying explicit statement that they are evil (e.g., homosexuality) makes them appear legitimate in the eyes of children and thus encourages experimentation. Consequently, it is improper even to consider certain subjects in public, regardless of the lack of information or the child's ignorance.

Because of their emphasis on management rather than libertarianism, advocates of sex education are by no means willing to tolerate all forms of sexual self-indulgence even by consenting adults.[14] Nonetheless, self-restraint versus self-indulgence becomes an issue, because the proponents are more reluctant to use the schools as means of explicitly limiting self-indulgence. Indeed, they are frightened by the idea of destroying the delicate balance between management and self-expression. To the opponents, the proponents' reluctance in fact legitimates immoral self-indulgence. School programs threaten certain moral precepts that must obviously be protected.

The School and Politico-Moral Conflict

At least since Plato, political elites have recognized the role that schools can play in the maintenance of social values. As a society becomes more complex and diverse, it can no longer depend upon the traditional agents of socialization to inculcate proper values and to sanction those who will follow or refuse to follow them. Thus, more impersonal institutions become important in communicating and enforcing these values. Such societies tend to depend to a greater extent on the school as an agent of social control. But what does social control mean in a society whose schools are supposedly dedicated to the inculcation of democratic values such as tolerance and diversity, as are the American schools? These schools are expected to teach an official or ideal culture whose norms are derived from a society that emphasizes democratic values and from an economic system that is based upon an extraordinarily high level of technology and corporate capitalism.[15] There is a tension between the need for diversity that democratic values encourage and the need for control that, as we previously mentioned, is an integral aspect in the maintenance of the social system.

The tension is nothing really new for the American public school, nor has the outcome of the tension necessarily stressed a commitment to democratic values to the degree that many defenders of the system have contended. Social control has been an integral goal of the American public school. As Horace Mann not at all reluctantly admitted in his defense of the free school, by means of such schools "the state shall have secured in all its children that basis of knowledge and morality, which is indispensable to its security."[16] In fact, throughout much of its history American education has maintained at best an ambivalence over whether to have solicitous concern for the maintenance of diverse moral views or whether to be more concerned with getting diverse subcultures to accept a more homogeneous morality.

This brief summary of the public school's role suggests some implications about the conflict over sex education. Political conflict seldom centers around the issue of whether or not the school should be used as an institution of social control. The battles have been over how much control and how successful the school might be. There have been basic conflicts over the *way* schools are to be used to inculcate these values. If the schools taught the more traditional morality, opponents of sex education would probably not object.

For the most part, the most visible proponents of school sex education represent or work for institutions that are primarily concerned with the delicate balance between the goals of self-expression and impulse control. These include various mental health organizations and, of course, the schools. They believe in the importance of both goals and have an abiding faith that their professions and the institutional context in which they operate can best cope with them.

Those favoring sex education in the schools are more willing to transfer the responsibility of much of sex education away from the family. They view the family as perhaps ideally the most proper source of sexual information, but insist that, like other subjects, sex and sexuality have become far too complex and technical to leave to the typical parent, who is either uninformed or too bashful to share useful sexual information with his child. Parents simply do not have the qualifications that a correctly trained schoolteacher has.

For three reasons they are not too concerned about removing certain aspects of sex education from the parents' domain. First, they minimize the conflict between school and parent and, indeed, are likely to advocate the preservation of the traditional family structure as an explicit goal.[17] Second, in this view, parents are not doing the appropriate job of sex education. Thus, on these matters the family is not very close-knit anyway. Finally, and most significantly, they believe that information furnished by school sex educators will liberate the parents from the discomfort of furnishing this information and allow the parents to do what they do best, the inculcation of specific moral values. In short,

A parent is too emotionally involved with his child to take a calm detached attitude toward that child's values and behavior or to be an objective educator. However, he does have the responsibility and the opportunity of inculcating the moral attitudes that will form the basic ethical framework for the child. No one can replace him in this task.[18]

It is on this issue of childrearing that the opponents feel most threatened. Mary Breasted argues that the proponents' view that parents were not qualified "to carry the full responsibility for the children's moral and sexual training ... [was] the real festering heart of [the opponents'] grievances."[19] These people see the destruction of traditional sources and strengths of parental influence as itself a grave threat to the maintenance of the traditional moral values. Sexual permissiveness is directly related to the degree to which modern society has separated its children from parental guidance and control. To the opponent of sex education, moral degradation is a direct result, or at least an indicator, of the lack of parental authority and respect that is rampant in this society. A policy that decreases the responsibility of the family is part of the problem and not part of the solution.

In order to understand this position and the sense of threat accompanying it, one must consider how opponents react to proponents' view of parental qualifications. This objection takes two forms. First, opponents quarrel with the proponents' view of what might be roughly called the quantity of information. Opponents argue that parents tell their children more than the proponents care to believe.

On a more sophisticated level, opponents also object to the belief that the school can act as a valid substitute for parental teaching about sex. If the school does not advocate a specific set of moral precepts, then it cannot complement the strength of parental authority. It can only work against this authority, because it combines an increase in information at the expense of the family, the proper source of influence. There is, in their view, no way that parental authority can undo this damage. They argue, moreover, that one must not assume that just because a child desires more information, it is proper for a schoolteacher to give it.

Policy Implications

Obviously, one characteristic of the conflict is that it is structured around the schools and thus involves those who normally make educational policy. But there are some broader implications that involve differences over the kinds of data that policy-makers can use and the kinds of sanctions that are acceptable to implement the policy decisions regarding the regulation of human sexual behavior.

The disagreement over conceptualization centers around the use of science and social science to inform decisions regarding public morality. The proponents' morality of consequences requires the use of scientific data because such information is a relatively effective means of forecasting and anticipating consequences. But science in general has a much more important function. "It is supposedly valuable in clarifying alternatives and determining cause-and-effect relationships, so that the various choice patterns will be evident."[20] Consequently, policy-makers should use such data as intelligence in developing their perceptions and attitudes about the nature of the sex education problem.

This view and its critics are clearly evident on the President's Commission on Obscenity and Pornography. Commissioners who advocated fewer laws against pornography, instead rely on sex education as the best means of developing a healthy attitude toward sex, claimed that they made these policy recommendations on the basis of empirical, scientific studies. They claimed to find little empirical evidence that showed ill effects of pornography and, as a result, recommended that most laws dealing with its regulation be eliminated. These empirical studies became their primary standard of evidence, and the commission placed the burden of proof on anyone who uses a different standard to measure propriety. "If a case is to be made against pornography in 1970," they confidently asserted, "it will have to be made on grounds other than demonstrated effects [i.e., empirical studies] of a damaging personal or social nature."[21] They do not, however, really recognize as legitimate any other way of making the case.

Relatively sympathetic commentators have raised serious questions about the strength of this empirical evidence used by the commission, but that is not an issue here.[22] What is important is that the opposition did not and does not accept these standards of evaluation in the first place. To them, the questions of sexual behavior are moral questions that *cannot* be dealt with by empirical scientific tests. On the surface, this view may appear to be narrow-minded, parochial, and intemperate, but it is quite consistent with the position that moral rules are relatively immutable and that their existence transcends human behavior. Thus, one turns not to science but religion to discover what is right for people to do. If one believes that God has conferred a fixed code of morality, then scientific standards are worse than irrelevant; they threaten the proper ethical and epistemological standards of a good society. This is a fundamentally divisive issue whose magnitude the proponents of sex education seem either to misunderstand or to ignore.

The intemperate, antiscientific, anti-intellectual tone of some of these objections should not becloud the fact that they raise an important and far-from-settled issue about the degree to which social scientific studies should inform public policy. The issue is far too complex to argue here in any complete form. We mention it only to preclude any attempt to dismiss these opposing arguments as useless and unprincipled merely because of their tone. One example will have to suffice. Edmond Cahn, in his discussion of *Brown v. Board of Education*, argues that there are some real costs in using social science to buttress what is essentially a moral position. Admittedly there are some important differences between sexual behavior and segregation: Cahn argues that the harm of segregation was easily seen and that there was a degree of moral consensus against its continued existence; no one could assert this about policies regarding sexual propriety. Nonetheless, his statement offers food for thought by looking at the question in a broader perspective than any that can be attributed to the partisans in the conflict over the regulation of sexual behavior:

It is one thing to use the current scientific findings, however ephemeral they may be, in order to ascertain whether the legislature has acted reasonably in adopting some scheme of social or economic regulation; deference here is shown not so much to the findings as to the legislature. It would be quite another thing to have our fundamental rights rise, fall, or change along the latest fashions of psychological literature. Today the social psychologists—at least the leaders of the discipline—are liberal and egalitarian (in basic approach). Suppose, a generation hence, some of their successors were to revert to the ethnic mysticism of the very recent past; suppose they were to present us with a collection of racist notions and label them "science"; What then would be the state of our constitutional rights?[23]

Proponents of sex education in the schools are much more willing to accept a combination of private and public sources of policy, but they stress the importance of the school. The proponents' view of the family's role in sex education is directly related to their attempts to separate facts from values in developing a pedagogy of sex education. Since the school should primarily teach a method of reaching decisions in sexual matters, it is possible to leave the more explicitly value-oriented teaching to church and family. The opposing view recognizes the need for some reeducative policy, but only at the private level, either through church or family. Even within this private realm, however, preferences are far more in the direction of the coercive. On the other hand, opponents most emphatically desire to adopt public policy as a means of coercing an individual to adopt a moral standard. For example, as the dissenting opinions of the President's Commission on Obscenity illustrate, opponents emphasize the use of the criminal sanction to regulate improper sexual behavior and actions that encourage such behavior.

The opponents seek to rely on the family as a source of sex education but depend upon the use of the criminal sanction as a supplementary means of gaining the child's respect for his parents' moral standards. In a sense, then, quite apart from its implementation, the criminal law is important to the opponents because it reinforces their view of sexual propriety when they attempt to influence their children. Thus, opponents use the law in a very real way, and school sex education policies supposedly compound the problem of defining right and wrong for their children. On the other hand, it is not so much that the proponents do not need the symbolic satisfaction of the criminal sanction. It is simply that the existence of the criminal law is far less important, and far more inimicable, to their moral values and related political objectives.

Moral Conflict and Political Conflict

We repeat that the preceding discussion merely states the value conflict in its most exaggerated form. Seldom, if ever, are political conflicts so clearly delineated on the basis of values. Indeed, much of the remainder of the book deals with the factors that keep the conflict from occurring in such potentially rancorous form. In the next chapter we deal more specifically with the methodological pitfalls of emphasizing value conflict. Nonetheless, at this stage, it is useful to suggest the potential these moral differences have for generating intense conflict.

If the opponents of sex education can convince a community that the issue involves a threat to its cherished moral values, then this group might indeed be able to derogate those active supporters of sex education. In a sense these opponents might then be able to argue that the normal rules of political discourse must be violated because of the stakes and the threat involved. There are, however, some strong community values to which the proponents can appeal in order to justify their attack on the opposition and make it more effective. For example, mental health professionals are frequently active proponents. These professionals have the special authority to label people as "fanatic." Because individuals frequently intermix fanaticism, mental illness, and moral divergence, seeing them all as a threat to stability, a moral position begins to be viewed as fanatic as it becomes less dominant. "Yesterday's moral virtue is today's ridiculed fanaticism."[24] Thus, the proponents may derogate by branding the opposition as an outgroup posing a serious threat to community values and stability. This can increase the degree of social and political control used against the opposition, which is stigmatized as not responsible for their dangerous actions.

Proponents of sex education also tend to derogate the opposition by arguing, perhaps unrealistically, that those opposing school sex education while intense in feeling, are few in number. For example, the President's Commission on Obscenity and Pornography reported that in a nationwide survey 58 percent of adult men and 54 percent of the women support without qualification sex education in the schools. Another 22 percent of the men and 23 percent of the women supported it with certain unstated qualifications, while about 15 percent of each group opposed it, and 7 percent had no opinion.[25] Other data from the Obscenity Commission-sponsored study, though less directly on point, support the idea of the existence of ambivalent attitudes toward changing sexual morality. Thirty-five percent of the sample would oppose the availability of pornography even if it were shown that the material was not harmful. Similarly, only 57 percent would sanction the availability of erotic material even if it were clearly shown that the material was not harmful.[26] In other words, a rather substantial minority (about 40 percent) oppose a morality of consequences when it comes to certain sex-related material. Those on the commission who favor sex education, however, used this poll as evidence of strong community support for sex education in the schools. But this interpretation is somewhat misleading.

Since only slightly more than half support such programs without qualifi- cations, it is certainly conceivable that an intense opposing minority could build a more broadly based coalition of opposition with those who lend only qualified support as well as take advantage of the degree of apathy. One should not play statistical tricks here; these findings tell us nothing about the actual policy- making process in a given community context. There can easily be a difference between abstract opinions and actions when one actually faces a concrete choice. Furthermore, a majority may not be necessary to affect the status of sex education. Nonetheless, we believe that the commission exaggerated when it cited this poll as overwhelming evidence that school sex education is opposed by only a small minority. At the very least this suggests a certain naïvete about the dynamics of community politics.

Moreover, as Table 1-1 shows, opposition to sex education did not decrease between 1943 and 1965. Indeed, opposition was as high in 1965 as it was in 1951, despite the fact that the question in the 1965 polls asks only about high-school programs, the kind that probably engender the most support. Again we must stress that these surveys do not by any means show overwhelming opposition, but they do suggest that proponents of sex education should be less euphoric or more cautious in their assessment of community support, and that they pay too little attention to community politics.

Thus, as presented, the value conflict discussion clearly lacks a dimension. It says virtually nothing about the dynamics of conflict and conflict avoidance. The actual strength of the opposition and the strength of the proponents require empirical investigation. In the next two chapters we suggest two common strategies of investigation that may be used to clarify the picture. The sociopsychological approach stresses value conflict with a more detailed analysis

Table 1-1
National Attitudes Toward Sex Education in the Schools, 1943-65

	1943 Poll[a]	1951 Poll[a]	1965 Poll[b]
Approve	67%	62%	69%
Disapprove	17	22	22
No Opinion	15	11	9
Other	1	4	–
N	(3093)	(1367)	(3499)

[a]Roper: "It has been suggested that a course in Sex Education be given to students in high schools. Do you approve or disapprove?"

[b]Roper: "Many schools give courses in Sex Education. Do you approve or disapprove of such courses?"

of the latent reasons for the political demands of the partisans. The other approach emphasizes the use of the theories of community conflict. We shall argue that the latter approach is more useful in answering some relevant questions about school sex education.

Sex Education:
The Orientation

The most vigorous proponents of school sex education are usually professionals in the educational or medical field: curricular specialists, school administrators, social workers, doctors, nurses, psychologists, and psychiatrists. Their most intense and visible opponents frequently have connections with the radical right. Antagonism between these groups is not surprising or new.

During the past few years the radical right has launched an intense and at times vicious attack against social and behavioral science. To some extent this can be attributed to a conflict of values. The radical rightists see behavioral science as a basic threat to their values, which include a more fundamental, clear, and certain distinction between good and evil. Furthermore, the rise in influence of behavioral science has made it more threatening to these rightists. The behavioral sciences have caught the public eye; they have become both more sophisticated and more a part of conventional wisdom. Institutions involving behavioral science personnel and techniques have become far more numerous and bureaucratic, and most important, they have become more directly involved in policy making, both at a national and local level.[1]

As we implied in Chapter 1, the proponents are accused of professional self-aggrandizement and advocacy of atheism and humanism; there are also charges that school and mental health professionals are leading us down the path toward one-world, Communist government. It is not surprising that the proponents' counterattack stresses the fanaticism and political deviance of the radical-right opposition. They are depicted as a hard core of uncompromising fanatics who dupe the average citizen into opposing sex education in the schools.

The proponents describe the opposition in terms of the psychological characteristics associated with politically deviant outgroups. Anti-sex-education campaigns are described as organized, well-financed movements led by small, cohesive groups whose deep-seated anxieties lead them to antidemocratic beliefs and to an ideological assault on our democratic system. The explanations emphasize the intractability of the opposition and their unwillingness to abide by the rules of the democratic game.[2]

What is most significant is that, despite disclaimers, this is the only view ever seriously considered in their writings on the subject. Occasionally, other sources and reasons for opposition are mentioned, but invariably these explanations are thrust aside in favor of psychopathology. For example, a psychiatrist commenting about the relationship among opposition to community mental health programs, opposition to sex education, and the behavior of the political right, went so far as to mention psychological studies that demonstrate the lack of abnormal amounts of psychopathology among ultraconservatives, but the remainder of his essay ignored this finding.[3]

This view of the radical right seems to coincide with conventional wisdom and, not surprisingly, with some important social theories. This conventional image of the radical right is so striking and deep-rooted that one must confront it prior to discussing any issue that involves such groups. One cannot discuss the radical right without confronting the argument that psychological characteristics are primary antecedents of radical-right behavior.

We contend that there are some very important limitations to this view; there is more to understanding the conflict over sex education than understanding the supposedly politically deviant or psychopathological characteristics of the opposition. In this chapter we shall illustrate the limits of this approach and pose an alternative that we shall subsequently use. For the sake of simplicity, we label the previously described view as "the psychological approach." The other may be called "the political conflict-social control approach," because it is more interested in conflict or lack of conflict and in policy making than it is in the psychological dimensions of the participants.[4]

The Psychological View

Joseph Gusfield's description of the values involved in politico-moral conflict is paradigmatic. Drawing upon his study of the temperance movement in the United States, he describes the basic conflict as one of values and their sources:

The cultural fundamentalist is the defender of tradition. Although he is identified with rural doctrines, he is found in both city and country. The fundamentalist is attuned to the traditional patterns as they are transmitted within family, neighborhood, and local organization. His stance is inward, toward his immediate environment. The cultural modernist looks outward, to the media of mass communications, the national organizations, the colleges and universities, and the influences which originate outside of the local community. Each sees the other in contrast. The modernist reveres the future and change as good. The fundamentalist reveres the past and sees change as damaging and upsetting.[5]

Our discussion in the first chapter suggests that the opponents of school sex education display many of the characteristics of the "fundamentalist" world view. The vocal opposition talks about the ways that school sex education threaten institutions that help maintain traditional values. But recognizing these similarities is not the same as accepting the value-conflict theory with all of its implications.

Gusfield's theories transcend the temperance movement.[6] We are less critical of his value-conflict approach than of the ways others have used it and similar approaches to describe the activities of the radical right. We do not question the association of these groups with a localistic point of view, although not enough general studies investigate this association with Gusfield's thoroughness. Our first objection is simply that those who follow Gusfield's approach tend to ignore a crucial portion of it by failing to consider the psychological characteristics of the modernist.

The dominant approach not only considers only one group, but also greatly limits the importance of the most visible characteristics in these culture conflicts. For example, the theories ultimately minimize the importance of the fundamentalist moral values. According to the prevailing theories, the traditionalists' grave concern with the deterioration of moral values in fact masks their greater and more basic, if less consciously recognized, concern with deterioration of their social status. Lipset and Raab take this position when they claim that the defense of the traditional moral position is merely the "baggage." What is really at stake is a way of life and the social position of those who subscribe to it.[7] The term "status politics" is frequently used to describe issues that on the surface involve defense of moral views but that in fact involve more basic concerns of life style.[8]

Since this view stresses the latent dimensions of the traditionalists' demands, these demands are viewed as symbolic of something else. They are considered expressive rather than instrumental. According to this approach, fundamentalist politics is less concerned with achieving concrete goals than with manifesting and reducing the latent frustrations that develop from efforts to maintain traditional values. In fact, the intensity of political demands is lessened not so much by the attainment of policy goals as by some formal declaration by public policy-makers that they are "dedicated" to achieving the goals.[9] What becomes important to the traditionalist is not so much that government implements a policy but that the government recognize and legitimate the traditionalists' frustrations. For example, Gusfield argues that the Women's Christian Temperance Union was less concerned with the implementation of prohibition laws than it was with their passage. To paraphrase Murray Edelman, this approach to the study of traditionalists tends to view their goals as forms of metaphors whose meaning changes as a function of the interests, hopes, and fears of the groups maintaining these views.[10]

Edelman's views are important here because he does not solely use these characteristics to describe the cultural fundamentalist, nor does he focus solely on traditional values. Both traditionalists and modernists are amenable to the manipulation of political symbols. Furthermore, he argues that the distinction between status and material issues is misleading.[11] The problem with the typical psychological approach is that it leaves the impression that political controversy pits an emotionally charged, politically irrational group of traditionalist extremists against rational, flexible modernists.

As a result, the usual psychopathological explanation is limited in its ability to view the political tactics of all the partisans. It tends to view the activities of the proponents of sex education as constantly defensive, always subject to the scurrilous and irrational attacks of the opposition. Again there is some truth to this explanation. A good portion of the opposition literature is intemperate and uses *ad hominem* arguments; literature favoring school sex education is usually introduced to a community only in response to opposition literature. Still, this explanation is one-sided, because these opposition groups are not the only ones who can derogate.[12]

If the opponents of sex education could convince a community that the issue involves a threat to its cherished moral values, then this group might indeed have this special ability to derogate those active supporters of sex education. In a sense these opponents might then be able to argue that the normal rules of political discourse must be violated because of the stakes and the threat involved.[13] As we mentioned in the previous chapter, however, some strong community values to which the proponents can appeal in order to justify their attack on the opposition and make it more effective.[14]

Psychological explanations fail to take adequate account of these and other political resources involved in community policy making. They offer little insight into the question of the strengths and weaknesses of groups that oppose sex education, nor do they consider the resources that policy-making elites can use to deal with such opposition.

More specifically, because the prevailing descriptions of the opposition characteristics so strongly stress the cohesiveness and single-minded dedication of these groups, these analyses tend to ignore a very important aspect of community power and community policy making. The success of groups opposing policy-making elites depends not merely upon their ability to oppose an issue publicly. Their success is also greatly affected by their ability to maintain constant vigilance over elite activity after the issue becomes less visible again. This form of political staying power depends upon the existence of a rather stable base of resources, in terms of time, money, as well as manpower. (We shall say more about this in the next chapter.) By implication, the typical analysis portrays the sex education policy-makers as vulnerable, defensive, and victimized. Certainly such a picture ignores much of what we know about community politics in general, and school politics in particular.

Gusfield tries to avoid these pitfalls. He recognizes that those who seek the prestige of public policy do so as a means of winning a political point, albeit a point that modernists may not find significant.[15] He also argues that if analysts recognize an issue as symbolic, they are better able to account for the zeal accompanying the issue and are less likely to brand political behavior as irrational or merely expressive. Our argument suggests a rather different conclusion: concern with the symbolic reinforces an emphasis on the expressive aspects of political behavior.

Regardless of the underlying reasons for moral positions, these views of morality help to set the tone and limits in which policy is made. Like other participants in the political process, those advocating this antimodernist position have a goal that may not in fact express latent interests but that does nonetheless help determine what the basic issues in a struggle over the adoption of public policy are going to be.

Psychopathological explanations are basically individualistic and emotive; they tend to attribute a set of beliefs to the personality of the individual. Thus, antidemocratic or antiscientific attitudes are seen as arising from a pathology in an individual's personality; these attitudes presumably satisfy some inner need. In this view, a person would oppose sex education because of some inner frustration or deprivation. This interpretation tends to underemphasize the relationship between perception and social structure. There is good evidence to show that beliefs have intellectual sources and psychological consequences rather than psychological sources and intellectual consequences. Thus, a person opposes diversity or modernity because of his lack of exposure to such ideas.[16] This distinction is more than academic. A cognitive explanation emphasizes sources of the intellectual development of the individual. It thus views the social and political milieu in which the individual lives as the most significant factors in understanding the development of belief systems.

Ours is not a study in individual psychology, so we cannot directly test for the relative strength of emotive versus cognitive factors. The implications of the emotive view are nonetheless important, because they suggest that the emphasis on psychopathology limits one's ability to see other important political aspects of the controversy. The nexus between social and political context and public policy making is all too easily ignored. We have already discussed the relationship between derogation and political conflict. There is little concern about the conflict-mitigating resources that educational policy-makers have at their disposal. This is perhaps the greatest of the limits to the psychological approach.

This is not to deny completely the usefulness of this approach. The issues it deals with are important and interesting, but they are limited or misleading in the assistance they give to answering some important questions:

1. Why did sex education become an issue?
2. Under what conditions does opposition to sex education develop?
3. Under what conditions does sex education fail to develop as a controversy?
4. What kind of school districts have such programs?
5. What are the political resources in the hands of both the proponents of sex education when the issue is raised in a community?
6. What is the relationship between school sex education policy making and educational policy making generally?
7. What effects, if any, does opposition have on the nature of sex education programs? Why is this the case?

8. What mechanisms do educational policy makers have at their disposal to counter the influence of the opposition?

The approach that we use, the political conflict approach, is geared to answer such questions.

The Political Conflict-Social Control Approach

The political conflict approach directs itself most specifically to the preceding questions, summarized in the general question: Why does conflict develop or fail to develop in a community, and what effect does the conflict have on the content of public policy? The psychological approach also speaks to the first question, but there are important differences between the two perspectives. The political conflict approach stresses the effect that the sociopolitical context has on the policy process. It is less interested in motivations or latent psychological dimensions than in the strategies used by the participants in policy making, the factors related to the choices of strategies, and the relationship between these strategies and policy content.

Our approach to the study of school sex education borrows freely from both empirical studies and theories of community conflict, including studies of educational policy making. Before developing the approach more specifically, we must list the operating assumptions and emphasis of our approach.

First, we see educational issues, including curricular ones, as being political in nature. So much has recently been written about the political nature of education decisions that we were tempted simply to make this contention without elaboration.[17] However, a few points apply rather specifically to the issue at hand. Whether politics is defined as "who gets what, when, and how" or as "the authoritative allocation of values," educational issues seem to fit the definition.[18] Curricular policy is no exception; it involves allocations of values and resources that have profoundly different implications for various social or cultural classes.[19]

The second operating characteristic is its emphasis on strategies rather than motives of the political actors involved. Again there are some important overlaps with the psychological approach. Theories of community conflict posit a relationship between distrust of political authorities and opposition to attempts at policy change. The community conflict approach is less concerned with the dimension of alienation from authority than with its manifestation.

Third, the approach considers the factors related to the choice of strategies in policy making. Which strategies reduce conflict? Which exacerbate it? Again psychological factors may be important, but again it is a question of emphasis. We focus on the more manifestly political phenomena, such as the nature and strength of authorities and opposition, as well as the resources available to them.

Finally, we consider the outcome of the strategy. Here we shall be concerned with both the content of the policies and with the development of the content. Why did some districts develop more comprehensive programs than did others? Why are some districts more innovative than others, and how, if at all, does innovativeness relate to sex education courses? A consideration of these questions is based on the assumption that the allocation of sex education programs is a political decision that, like other such decisions, is greatly dependent upon the dynamics of the community's educational policy making process. It assumes that latent psychological factors, whether or not they are "moral baggage," are mitigated by the social and political context.

A complete look at school sex education would require a more systematic synthesis of the two approaches than we can offer here. We contend that our emphasis makes it easier to deal with the important questions that we raised and that the users of the psychological approach have carelessly overextended its use. In the following chapter we elaborate our approach, but at this stage it is important to note that our emphasis has shifted toward the view of school policy-makers as authorities who have a great deal at their disposal to mitigate conflict and that such conflict mitigation (or social control) is crucial to our approach.

Community Educational
Policy Making

The most common question about school sex education—"Why did it become an issue?"—serves as a useful guide to our investigation, because it suggests an important double meaning of the word *issue*. First, the word implies visibility and importance; one is really asking why sex education became visible, who determined that there was a need for it, and who objected. Second, the word *issue* connotes conflict, as when someone says, "Why are they making such an issue of the situation?" Both meanings of the word play an important role in the schoolman's occupational life.[1] On the one hand, he is expected to convince his clientele or his constituents of their needs and, indeed, to define their needs for them. He is supposed to make his own ideas visible and convince others of their worth. We shall subsequently show that this need creation may be the most important aspect of the predominant, normative model that guides school policy making. On the other hand, school professionals, like other policy-makers, are acutely aware of the fact that policy making can be accompanied by visibility and controversy that not only threaten the success of a specific policy but also threaten their authority and careers.

Thus, our approach to the study of school sex education stresses the techniques by which schoolmen handle the tensions between innovation and conflict. On the basis of this discussion of tensions we shall offer a set of hypotheses to be investigated in subsequent chapters.

The approach focuses on the school superintendent. The superintendent is, by definition, the chief executive officer of a district and responsible for its policies and programs. Though there have been recent increases in factors that tend to narrow their discretion, educational politics, especially in curricular matters, is still basically controlled by the school professional.

Also, the focus is useful from a methodological standpoint, because there is ample reason to believe that the qualities of the superintendent represent qualities the board desires for its district. The superintendency is a focal position in the district. In choosing a superintendent, the board must rely upon its own assessment of the manner in which a potential superintendent will behave. Its criteria for selection roughly represents an ideal view of the district's expectations, values, or goals in the field of education.

Educational Innovation

When a school district adopts a curriculum change, it is involving itself in policy innovation. Accordingly, the literature on the diffusion of innovation is quite relevant to an understanding of curricular change. This literature suggests that two crucial aspects are involved in innovation: the nature of the social system in which innovation is diffused, and the visibility and importance of the issue for those potentially involved in making the change.

Everett M. Rogers has suggested that innovation takes place within "situational fields" and is "normatively regulated."[2] "Situational field" refers to the social system within which the innovation is diffused, i.e., a set of mechanisms that serves to transmit the innovation between various actors.

In social systems, the interaction between those involved is normally in the form of communication. Information channels are therefore a major component of the situational field. Innovators are well attuned to the communications system diffusing information about the innovation. Both the availability of information about the innovation in cosmopolitan sources and the innovator's readiness to look to those sources are important. There may be information about sex education in cosmopolitan media, but those in the local district may either not be exposed to it or may not view the media as credible.

Innovation is "normatively regulated"; potential innovators must evaluate their own behavior in such a way that consideration of an innovation is important to them. If so, an innovator's behavior is regulated by norms emphasizing the importance of innovation per se. The groups to which *potential innovators* refer for norms regulating their behavior generally must approve of innovation in general and of the specific innovation in order for them to become *actual innovators*. In short, innovation will not take place unless there exist both a perceived need for it and norms creating a favorable orientation toward it. We turn now to a more detailed discussion of variables that can be expected in these situational and normative fields.

Professionalization of education administration seems to be a crucial correlate of curricular innovation. A profession may be thought of as a cosmopolite source of information. It extends the range of contacts for its practitioners beyond their local environment. Thus, the situational field does not simply include elements in the local district. It also includes a social system—the education profession—which connects a number of local units. Hence, the school district is only an element in this broader social system. In the majority of cases, superintendents are not locally oriented. They are outsiders to the communities in which they work, at least in the sense that they are relatively recent arrivals. We found that very few of the superintendents who responded to our questionnaire had built their careers in their current districts. Only 15 percent of the superintendents reported that their first job had been in the district where they were then employed. Approximately 29 percent had started careers in a different state, and 56 percent in the same state but a different district. More than 50 percent reported that their previous job had been in a different school district, 17 percent in a different state and 38 percent in the same state. In addition, 53 percent reported that they had been superintendent in at least one other school district.

In short, school superintendents are not simply successful members of the local educational community. They are, instead, highly mobile members of a profession. Advanced academic training is a normal prerequisite to passage into a profession. The necessity for advanced training has been well established in public education. All but one percent of our superintendent respondents had a master's degree, and 62 percent had majored in educational administration. Fifty-eight percent held doctoral degrees, and 87 percent of these were in educational administration. With such professional training, superintendents owe much of their success and allegiance to their profession, not to the district in which they are currently employed. When a school board sets about to hire a new superintendent, it usually establishes a screening committee of *professional* educators to provide an initial evaluation of *professionally trained* candidates and to weed out those candidates who do not come up to *professional* standards.

Despite the similarity in credentials, schoolmen still differ in their responses to innovation, because all are not equally attuned to the relevant communication processes. The profession serves as the carrier of important information to its practitioners through a variety of formal and informal methods. Probably most important are the professional journals. These act as important carriers of innovations by transmitting new ideas and relating these ideas to the proper vocational activities of practitioners. For example, the reader of professional educational publications is quickly impressed by the variety of new methods for teaching existing subjects, laying out and using school space, and developing programs. The amount of interchange among profession members in the journal articles is also impressive.

A more important function performed by the professional journals is *generating* the need for the program. We will have more to say about this when discussing the role of the profession in providing the local administrator with normative guidance. However, consider for a moment the idea that this profession, through its publications, creates the need for curricular innovation, that is, its members become interested in change and try to convince others that this change interest is a legitimate and important one. There is also a normative dimension here. The analogy between curricular innovation and advertising is helpful. The education profession may help to create that need by "advertising" curricular change in its literature. However, the "advertising" would not be effective unless school administrators were attuned to that literature, unless they saw it as a source of authoritative guidance. At this point professionalization enters the picture again.

An organized profession does not exist merely to provide advice to its members; it also provides a status structure within which the competence of the practitioners is formally and informally evaluated. To achieve such status, the novitiate models his conduct after that prescribed by other members of his profession. Crain et al. report that more professionally oriented city managers, those who sought the approval of other city managers rather than just local leaders, were more likely than less professionally oriented managers to support fluoridation of water supplies. Fluoridating the water supply was an innovation that the professional manager was expected to carry out.[3]

These innovation-oriented factors come together in the school professional's model of behavior, which stresses the need for professional autonomy and narrowly limits the legitimate channels that lay people may use to affect the policy process. Dale Mann calls this the "public relations" model and finds it predominant in theory and practice among educational professionals. We shall subsequently consider the extent of its prevalence, but first it is necessary to describe this model:

1. A stress on one-way communication. School professionals are obliged to communicate their decisions to the public, but the emphasis is definitely on citizen cooperation rather than citizen participation.
2. A stress on getting the citizen to support the policy as it is defined by the school professional.
3. A view of citizens as consumers, with the closely related view that among the citizenry there is a basic consensus about the goals of education and the means to achieve them. Disagreement with the goals is seldom recognized as legitimate.
4. A final and all-important emphasis on professional autonomy. This last line of defense stresses the technical, esoteric nature of education.[4]

The public relations ideology is readily apparent in the school administrator's primary reference sources. These norms are reflected by specialized publications, by peer groups that he contacts either formally (e.g., at a convention) or informally, and by other sources of information about professional developments. Such reference sources not only stress their special competence and expertise but also imply that a professionally oriented superintendent must maintain a certain independence from his community. Indeed, at times he must be willing to advocate a position even if unpopular with the community. In this view, since superintendents can best define educational needs, particularly in curriculum and administration, they must remain somewhat aloof from community demands. In their interviews with Massachusetts school superintendents, Gross, Mason, and McEachern found that both superintendents and board members expected the former to represent "educational principles or methods" to the public. Seventy-eight percent of the superintendents felt that the superintendent absolutely must "fight continuously against any local attacks on educational principles or methods which he knows to be sound."[5]

This public relations model has implications for educational policy-makers' views on lay participation that are aptly illustrated in the following statements by authors quite explicitly instructing school professionals in policy strategy:

The authorization of [lay] committees and the policy under which they will work should be the responsibility of the Board of Education along with the Superintendent of Schools.

An advisory committee must be oriented from the beginning to recognize that its advice does not constitute interference with the workings of the legal organization: on the contrary, it insures a greater amount of invulnerability in the functioning of the entire school organization.[6]

Because this model is obviously meant to guide the school professionals' everyday activity, we might expect that those most attuned to the norms of the profession would generally try to be the most innovative. There is some general evidence for this. From a review of the evidence, Everett M. Rogers concludes, "It is doubtful whether an individual who is an innovator for one idea is a laggard for another idea."[7] Further, Richard O. Carlson reports that the superintendents who adopted his selected innovations were generally more cosmopolitan and professionally oriented.[8] But what of the costs of innovation? Innovations entail risk for the policy-maker. Surely this must be part of his decision-making calculus, and thus our approach must also consider possible costs.

Community Educational Policy Making

Something rather paradoxical about local educational policy making must be considered at this point. On the one hand, the ways by which such policies are generally made suggest that in the active policy-making process the public relations model is successfully implemented. One set of characteristics suggests that such policy making is typically consensual, with little mass participation. This is particularly true in curricular matters. School policies are made by a rather well-entrenched elite, whose members accept very similar norms about the local educational policy process. These norms grant much discretion and control to the local schoolman.[9] A recent survey of the literature characterized school policy making, especially in regard to curriculum, as a process in which the school professionals "define alternatives, produce resources, provide specific policy making recommendations, and recommend the formal agenda."[10] To the extent that professionals share involvement with other groups or individuals, they tend to be not only generally supportive of professional discretion but also of the general policy-making norms. The increased involvement of the federal government in educational policy making, whether desegregation or grants-in-aid, has limited such discretion, but the evidence nonetheless rather convincingly shows that the local schoolman still has great control over community educational policies.[11]

The schoolman's professional reference groups stress the need for innovation and the necessity of convincing the community that these innovations are essential. Need generation is viewed as an important, if not the most crucial, aspect of school professionals' work. Indeed, the journals whose readership is presumably from this group quite clearly associate innovation with professionalization. A good school superintendent keeps abreast of new educational innovations and effectively convinces his community that it is in its interest to adopt the innovation.

Of course, this relationship between professionalization and innovation does not apply solely to the education policy process, but it seems a particularly important aspect here because it so nicely dovetails with the low-key, professional discretion, consensual setting in which much policy is generally made. These two aspects of the setting reinforce each other. The control maintained by school professionals makes it easier for them to define community educational needs and to develop, as well as implement, policies geared to meet these needs. By accepting the legitimacy of the schoolman's professionalism, the community helps to establish an important basis of the schoolman's authority.

But conflict exists, even if it is not endemic or typical. The tension lies in these situations because, despite the great stress upon innovation and the existence of norms and resources conducive to it, the political costs of innovation can be extraordinarily great for the schoolman.

When conflict does develop, it tends to be unanticipated.[12] School professionals are surprised at the opposition and controversy engendered over what they viewed as a simple, noncontroversial, apolitical matter. Too, the issues themselves frequently involve what Agger and Goldstein call "cultural class conflict." Positions on the issues reflect basic differences in attitudes and perspective concerning the public interest, the community and its problems, and innovation in policy making.[13] In short, school conflicts are frequently manifestations of broader issues that involve a perceived threat to some groups' moral principles.

In addition to substantive policy, conflicts tend to involve issues of authority and political participation. In this regard the involvement of the radical right is important. Agger and Goldstein feel that the perspective of the radical right in educational matters renders them "at all times a potential participant in policy making involving changes deemed necessary or useful by educational experts for 'pedagogical' reasons."[14] School policy making elites are by no means unabashedly liberal; they are probably slightly to the right of center.[15] Nonetheless, even the more conservative members of the elite are not at all amenable either to the radical right's interest in defining educational issues as political ones or to their desire to limit the scope of school professional expertise. It is among radical-rightists that the professional's scope of curricular authority is most severely questioned.[16]

The issues in these conflicts typically involve not just the content of the policy but also the basic norms and procedures used by elites to make it. They are conflicts between these elites, along with their "responsible" constituencies that accept the legitimacy of schoolmen's authority, and the "outsiders," who question the basis of professional expertise and the limited extent of mass participation.[17] Radical-right groups are typically outsiders regarding both education and other issues.

According to William Gamson, conflicts are rancorous when they are characterized by a belief that the norms of waging political conflict have been violated. This contrasts to conventional conflict, where established and accepted means of political expression are used and opponents regard each other as having mistaken but still legitimate goals.[18] Because of the authority and participation issues, educational conflict typically falls on the rancorous side. The legitimacy of the opposing views is not accepted.

Finally, educational conflict tends to be episodic and quixotic. It typically disappears almost as rapidly as it arises. Admittedly, this is the riskiest generalization we have made so far. Conflicts over one issue frequently tend to build coalitions that carry over to other issues.[19] Still, two recent studies of educational policy making suggest that there are difficulties in maintaining such coalitions. In their investigation of response to the U.S. Supreme Court's school prayer decisions, Dolbeare and Hammond show that the tightly controlled nature of everyday school policy making and its lack of public visibility make surveillance of schoolmen's activities rather difficult for opposing groups. Merely to overcome the usual degree of community apathy requires a great allocation of psychic and economic resources. Often there are few resources left afterward.[20] With more direct evidence, Agger and Goldstein demonstrate that in Eugene, Oregon, radical-right groups did not succeed in developing cross-issue support even though these groups seemed instrumental in bringing about a referendum defeat of something as basic as an annual school district budget.[21]

Let us summarize the contradictions. Conflict is not very frequent, yet its occurrence is rather unpredictable. Extreme calm is replaced by rancor. There seems to be an extreme fluctuation from apparently strong consensus to intense disagreement over substance and procedure. Educational policy making is typically developed from the top down, yet school conflict frequently involves not merely a substantive issue but also the basic issue of the degree of citizen participation allowed in policy formulation. Patterns of authority, which are usually stable, also come under direct attack. Thus, while there is a strong pressure for innovation, there are unpredictable but possibly high costs in pursuing this change.

Policy-Making Techniques

How, if at all, do policy-makers deal with these tensions? Mann implies that conflict results from the schoolman's use of the public relations model, which decreases his ability to recognize or anticipate conflict. Though the blinders created by this behavior are undoubtedly a factor, we believe that Mann's explanation of conflict is incomplete.[22] It fails to account adequately for schoolmen's behavior in dissensual policy-making situations. On the basis of Mann's analysis, we might thus assume that when the schoolman faces dissensus and conflict he has only the model to follow. Mann fails to consider other strategies the schoolman might have at his disposal.

Another variation upon which one might build a theory stresses the constraints that conflict—or its anticipation—places on the schoolman's policy making. Dolbeare and Hammond argue that conflict avoidance is the primary goal of schoolmen, at least in the five relatively small towns and cities in their study.[23] When conflict develops, a school professional may discover that dissonance exists between his normative policy-making model, which stresses professional autonomy and distrust of citizen participation, and the need to allow such participation on the part of the obstreperous opposition. Dissonance might be resolved by what Frederick Wirt calls a "hot potato ploy." The schoolman redefines the issue as "political" rather than "educational." Consequently, it is no longer within his domain and hence requires nonprofessional, i.e., lay citizen, decision making. This is in a sense conflict avoidance by abdication.

This view also is limited, because, like Mann's approach, it fails to consider the *range* of conflict-mitigating strategies at the disposal of the schoolman. Both lean too far in the direction of assuming that opposition to regular school policy making, though infrequent, cripples the policy-makers.

Our own approach tries to combine other possible strategies into an integral part of the explanation. It assumes that schoolmen do indeed want to avoid conflict, that they sense some of the contradictions and tensions we have described, and that in fact they feel some cross-pressure about innovations. It also assumes that they try to resolve the pressures by hedging against loss of professional autonomy without succumbing too much to the citizenry. Most important, it attempts to strike a balance by stressing the policy-making elites' discretion, while recognizing the fact that their own strategies are somewhat constrained.[24]

There are sound theoretical reasons for viewing the schoolman in this light. William Gamson suggests that conflict and its resolution generally has this kind of dynamism. Using Gamson's approach, we view the schoolman as an authority who seeks to control the degree of influence of "those actors who for a given decision, are affected by the authority in some 'significant' way."[25] Gamson calls these actors "potential partisans." Authorities are both potentially the recipients or targets of influence and the agents of social control whose aim is to counter or limit this influence. Gamson aptly describes this process as the "management of discontent."

There are basically two techniques by which discontent can be managed. The schoolman authority can alter the content of a decision, or he can make an effort to limit the source of pressure by using the strategies of counterinfluence on the partisans.[26]

Though our approach stresses counterinfluence, a word must be said about altering the content of a policy. Most simply, content can be altered by initially presenting a policy and then adjusting it to the responses of the community. Policy-makers can also use variations of this strategy by anticipating community reactions and then introducing policies with contents that try to avoid the objections they anticipated. Regardless of strategy, in this context the most important thing to remember about content alteration is that some policies are much more amenable to alteration than are others. Policies differ in the degree to which their content can be adjusted without destroying the integrity of the program. For example, under present levels of technology, a community must either fluoridate all its water or none. It simply cannot avoid imposing fluoridation upon those who do not want it. On the other hand, curricular policies can be changed in a variety of ways in response to community demands. The grades at which an innovation is to be introduced can be modified, programs might be made optional rather than required, and some subject matter can be eliminated or otherwise modified.

Counterinfluence strategies allow the schoolman to deal with opposition without necessarily altering the content of the policy. Choice of specific methods of counterinfluence depend upon the strength of the opposition. Generally, the greater the pressure by partisans, the broader is the base of citizen participation that the schoolman must allow. The degree of opposition is directly related to the unpredictability of the social control strategy that the schoolman chooses. This strategy may appear irrational, but given the characteristics of the educational policy process, it is not. If he attempts to circumvent heavy opposition by using policy-making techniques that ignore their interest in participating, he may win an award for bravery, and he may even succeed: however, he runs the very real risk of exacerbating the basic and most threatening authority-participation issues. It thus seems plausible to expect that he would try to strike some kind of balance. These strategies may be seen as a continuum of increasing involvement by citizens. Along that dimension are such techniques as holding a public referendum, holding a public meeting to discuss policy, appointing various forms of committees to develop policy, and making policy unilaterally, i.e., without the use of committees or meetings.

Public Referenda

The referendum encourages the widest amount of citizen participation. But it is also an unpredictable strategy for achieving the superintendent's policy goals, because it requires developing new working arrangements and new forms of accommodation and because it involves people who do not regularly make policy. Under most circumstances, the superintendent is not likely to believe that the structure of the referendum, with its all-or-nothing alternatives and its "uninformed" participants, is conducive to policy making. Unless it is required by law, the use of the referendum strategy is a sign that those who opposed the existing or proposed educational policies have gained the upper hand.

Holding a Public Meeting

This strategy is more acceptable than a referendum, because the administrator has a greater chance of control over agenda and alternatives. This public forum also has a certain appeal as a solution to innovation-conflict dilemma, because it gives the school administrator an apparent means of consulting with parents without giving up all control over the issues.

Nonetheless, such meetings can' present serious threats to his goals. With this strategy, the administrator provides the opposition with a platform for airing its disagreement. This forum also gives other important advantages to the opposition, especially if it is an intense minority. There is a good chance that these opponents will be overrepresented at such meetings, especially since they may try to pack them. School policy makers fear that their supporters will become intimidated by the active opposition. In another subtle but important way, the success of public meetings is problematical, because the partisans whom the schoolman seeks to control may ultimately feel that the tolerance of policy-makers was at best patronizing or at worst deceitful.

The Strategic Use of Committees

Neither referendum nor public meeting offers the optimal mix of innovation, participation, and conflict resolution. Each of these strategic methods absorbs new elements into the policy process, but each fails to do so in a way likely to minimize conflict. The use of a committee, however, affords the best opportunity both to include new or irregular participants in the process and to control the outcome. Appointing a committee allows the policy-maker to take the heat off himself, to appeal to democratic values by considering other viewpoints in a way that seemingly gives them a chance to be consequential, to co-opt the advocates of opposing viewpoints, and still to keep a commitment to innovation. Optimally, the strategy gives the layman some voice in the matter yet still provides enough control of policy making to guarantee the results desired by policy-makers.

This alternative has much to recommend it as a method for exercising counterinfluence by co-opting the opposition, for, within limits, the schoolman can control its membership.[27] The committee can be selected to include school officials and "respected members of the community" who are initially predisposed toward the administration's position. Moreover, by including moderate leaders of the opposition, the administration can moderate the amount of disagreement in committee discussions, yet use the opposition members as opinion spokesmen in a specialized part of the community. The simple act of establishing the committee may create the illusion of community participation in policy making. Participation may also reduce opposition by developing more acceptance of operating rules, thereby both increasing predictability and reducing rancor.

In the real world of school politics, however, things seldom work that way. Like all other strategies, the success of the committee-co-optation strategy is problematical. It is difficult to limit the influence that the co-opted elements may have on the policy process once they are included. The balance and composition of the committees are initially the critical factors. Committees composed entirely of lay persons would seem to be related to the highest level of opposition among districts using committees. Next, in decreasing order, would be committees composed of both lay persons and school professionals, or others who regularly participate in educational policy making, and finally, committees composed entirely of professionals and regular participants.

In fact, this relationship is probably not unilateral or simple, because the lay person/professional committee is best suited for controlling the opposition by co-optation. It comes closest to the optimal combination of having enough of the regular participants in the policy-making structures and process to retain control, and yet still being able to defend itself against the accusations that it is controlled or even dominated by these elements. A committee composed entirely of the professionals and school board members—the more regular participants in policy making—might easily agree without conflict but find that this policy is far from acceptable to the community. In contrast, a committee composed entirely of lay persons is less familiar with, or less willing to accept, the dominant premises, procedures, or goals of those who normally make educational policy. Thus, while we would anticipate that there is a generally direct relationship between opposition strength and the amount of lay representation on committees, we must also consider that the more professionally oriented committees, which schoolmen are sorely tempted to use, are easily prone to tactical error.

Unilateral Policy Making

Here policy making is carried out only by the regular educational policy-makers through existing procedural channels and structures. No committees are appointed, no public meetings are called, and no referenda are held. Dolbeare and Hammond describe a similar situation:

Through intra-elite communication channels, negotiations take place between those most deeply affected by forthcoming matters and an accommodation generally acceptable to all is worked out and instituted into the official arenas of decision-making. Thus, most issues in effect have been acted upon by the power structure before they ever come to public notice.[28]

Bureaucratization of conflict is another variation of unilateral policy making.[29] It is unilateral in the sense that conflict is finally resolved by an organization that is isolated from opposition influence and is under more direct control of the schoolman. In short, the issues in conflict become routinized, and "political" issues become "apolitical" or "educational" again. This conflict-mitigating mechanism may not be apparent in the early stages of policy making. Indeed, it may not arise until after the strategies more oriented to mass participation has been used. Final policy development and implementation are then referred to a bureaucratic organization where they can remain until the issue cools down. Important policy changes can then be made at this level, especially if schoolmen can argue, "We let the community decide the basic issues. Now we are simply applying our expertise to the question." Our earlier discussion of educational conflict suggests that some opposition groups display more than a touch of cynicism about such arguments. However, one must remember that another characteristic of educational conflict—the opposition's lack of staying power—increases the likelihood that bureaucracies can not only mitigate conflict but also reintroduce outcomes that were altered in response to pressure.

Local Educational Policy Making:
Some Hypotheses

We can summarize this entire discussion in the form of hypotheses that ought to apply to educational policy making, especially curricular matters.

Professionalization and Innovation

Hypothesis A-1. The need for innovation is generated from within the education profession.

Hypothesis A-2. The generation of this need is accompanied by an emphasis on the authority of schoolmen to carry out such innovations.

Hypothesis A-3. Districts with more professionalized schoolmen are quicker to consider and adopt innovations.

Hypothesis A-4. School districts that are generally more innovative are quicker to consider and adopt new programs.

Conflict Resolution Strategies
and Policy Output

Hypothesis B-1. Sex education policies, like other curricular programs, are very amenable to content-alteration strategies.

Hypothesis B-2. The degree of opposition to a proposed sex education policy is directly related to the amenability that a policy-making forum has for citizen involvement.

Hypothesis B-3. The less amenable the policy-making mechanisms to citizen involvement, the more comprehensive is the policy content.

In the next chapter we begin to investigate the hypotheses regarding innovation and professionalization. Chapter 5 looks at the hypotheses involving conflict resolution strategies and policy output; it is concerned with the success of the opposition. Chapter 6 attempts to take a closer look at the linkage between innovation and counterinfluence.

Professionalization and Innovation

We turn in this chapter to the hypotheses concerning the sources of demands for sex education (see hypotheses A1-A4 in Chapter 3). We then look at the relationship between level of professionalization and amenability to sex education programs. Finally, we investigate the links between a district's general propensity to innovate and its willingness to consider these programs. We do not intend to imply a conspiratorial role for the education profession; there is no single group or single opinion within the profession concerning the utility value of sex education. We discuss general tendencies. When we describe the profession as exerting pressure on its members to support sex education, we refer to informal peer pressure. What in fact seems to exist is great agreement among professional educators that sex education should be made a part of the regular curriculum of school districts. While agreement is reflected in the professional publications and is made known through them, this is certainly not a conspiracy.

If we grant that there may be an objective need for the schools to offer sex education as part of their regular curriculum, then we have to ask why now and not fifty years ago. One reason may be the politico-moral changes discussed in Chapter 1. Some will argue that the need did not exist earlier, that times have changed and the church and family are no longer fulfilling their roles in this area. This may be true, but it still does not explain why so many school systems found it necessary to implement family life/sex education programs at approximately the same time, unless the stimulus arose from outside the community's notion of its needs, i.e., from the school profession.

The Generation of Need

Proponents of sex education tend to view the development of these programs as responses to public demands. For example, an article supporting the introduction of sex education claims, "There was a public demand in many [New Jersey] communities for the schools to assume more responsibility in preparing children and youth for effective home life."[1] We have no data that can be applied directly to the New Jersey case, but our own findings suggest that the proponents' interpretation can be challenged.

It is necessary to consider two questions about the development of the need for sex education. From which sources did the need arise? What was the rationale used by those advocating this innovation? Our answers to these questions are based on information culled from an investigation of sex education literature, the time of its publication, and the relationship between the availability of these materials and the time when sex education was actually considered by the various school districts.

In our study of the literature we focus on the role of journal articles as agents of diffusion, because they seem most available to any potential innovators. To trace the history of interest in sex education in both the public and in the education profession, we counted articles in three different types of publications for a twenty-year period from 1950 through 1969. To measure public interest in education, two sources were searched: *The New York Times Index* and *The Readers' Guide to Periodical Literature.* The *New York Times* is a source of general news aimed at a lay audience. However, its audience is probably better educated than the general population of the United States. *The Readers' Guide to Periodical Literature* indexes articles from various sources and does not direct itself to any specialized segment of the population. To determine the amount of interest that professional educators had in sex education during this period, we examined the *Educational Index.*

The hypothesis that the education profession is the initial source of interest in sex education can be tested by comparing the time when articles on sex education appeared in professional periodicals to the time when districts considered sex education. If articles appeared in large numbers before large numbers of districts considered (but not necessarily adopted) sex education, then we have some suggestive, but not conclusive, evidence supporting the hypothesis. Of course, it is also possible that articles in education periodicals reflected the already existing interests of their readers. In that case, large numbers of districts should have started considering sex education prior to the appearance of a large number of articles in the education periodicals.

We found that public interest and concern about sex education followed after the initial activities of school professionals. As the data from Table 4-1 show, the majority of the articles in professional journals appeared before 1964. However, most school districts did not consider the program in great numbers until the period 1965-68, and the general public did not demonstrate a great deal of interest in the subject until 1969.

The proportion of articles per year (mean yearly percent) in professional publications increased during the 1965-68 period, but at nowhere near the rate of district consideration of sex education. The average number of articles per year in professional publications, from 1950-64 to 1965-68, increased by a factor of approximately two, while the average number of considerations per year increased by a factor of eight.

Discussion of school sex education by those outside the education profession seemed more a reaction to, than a cause of, these programs' consideration by school districts. Nearly one-half (45 percent) of the articles in lay periodicals appeared during 1969. This antedates the period of heaviest district consider-

Table 4-1

Interest in Sex Education in the Education Profession and the Public and the Year It Was First Considered by School Districts

	Years that Articles in Specialized Periodicals Appeared		Years First Considered By School Districts		Years that Articles in Lay Readership Appeared	
	Percent	Mean Yearly Percent	Percent	Mean Yearly Percent	Percent	Mean Yearly Percent
1950-64	54	3.4	30	2.0	20	1.3
1965-68	32	8.0	64	16.0	35	8.5
1969	14	(14.0)	6	(6.0)	45	(45.0)
	$N = 366$		329		123	

37

ation of sex education and probably reflects public concern about programs that had been, or were, in the process of being implemented. We infer that public activity was typically a response to a subject already well considered and advocated by the education profession. The thrust and source of need generation becomes clearer with a closer look at the content of the professional journals' sex education literature. It is, above all else, hortatory, stressing the view of experts and professional autonomy.

The Content of the Professional Literature

Approximately one quarter (88) of the sex education articles appearing in education and related professional journals were read and their content analyzed. The coders were instructed to develop a set of categories that would summarize the content of the articles. They were also instructed to note especially whether the content of the article supported sex education, opposed sex education, or was affectively neutral toward it. *None* of the articles appearing in education journals fell into the anti-sex-education category. There were no real debates on the merits of the idea.

Pro Sex Education

Articles in this category tended to emphasize the general need for sex education. Sex education, according to these articles, is a necessary function of the schools because other sources have failed to meet their responsibilities. Sex education will reduce ignorance about sexual matters, instill students with a moral code, and increase their potential for personal fulfillment. Forty-eight percent of the articles in professional journals were in this pro-sex-education category.

Two characteristics stand out. First, there is great emphasis on the fact that appropriate authorities and reference groups of school professionals unequivocally support the programs. For example, in 1966 and again in 1969, *Nation's Schools*, a journal for school administrators, published short articles on opinion polls dealing with sex education. The respondents were all "school administrators." These polls reported that about one-third of the respondents had sex education programs in their districts. This small percentage was not seen as manifestation of community sentiment but rather as a challenge to school professionals: "Approximately two-thirds of schoolmen polled this month didn't have a sex education program in their districts—but it's not because they don't think they need one."[2] About 55 percent of our sample had sex education programs. This disparity may be attributed to the fact that we sampled only relatively large districts. *Nation's Schools'* response rate for both of these polls was approximately 50 percent, which compares favorably with our response rate outside of the South. Interestingly, *Nation's Schools'* response rate seems to be about 60 percent when the questionnaire deals with subjects other than sex education. The 1969 article reported that 70 percent of the administrator respondents thought that their districts "should" have sex education programs.[3] Statements supporting sex education usually contain one or another of the following statements as verification: "Most authorities today feel . . . " or "Most experts maintain. . . ." Or they cite the support of prestigious organizations, as in the following circular argument: "That the need for responsible sex education by trustworthy sources is imperative has been recognized . . . by at least 17 national organizations that support sex education in schools."[4]

The second important characteristic is the lack of systematic empirical evidence to support the value of school sex education. Two of the articles were based on data gathered from students. One of those indicated that a small sample of students who had taken sex education liked it and thought it useful.[5] The other was a study of the sexual attitudes of teenage girls. It concluded that parents were not doing the job properly.[6] This study gives no direct evidence about whether school sex education can pick up the slack. The rest of the surveys were directed toward either teachers or administrators and dealt with whether or not they had sex education in their schools or wanted it in their schools. There was no report of an independent evaluation of the programs.

More typical was the press release by the National Educational Association. The NEA described the program as one "that has been of great value to millions of school children over the years and particularly during the 1960's when more and more schools added sex education to their curriculums."[7]

Unlike supporters of fluoridation, proponents of sex education can point to no body of impressive scientific evidence analyzing the effects of their proposed innovation. This lack of evidence increases the pressure to place one's faith in the opinion of the experts.

The existence of scientific evidence, however, does not guarantee that it will be effective in community conflict, as the fluoridation controversy demonstrated. Despite that fact that the experts cited such evidence to show that fluoridation was beneficial, the average citizen frequently refused to accept these findings. This refusal was not based so much upon irrationality as it was upon the fact that the opponents' view of fluoridation was so frightening, the citizen chose to hedge his bets. In the view of the average person, his or her teeth were not so bad, and a few cavities were worth risking, given the possibility that the opponents' view of fluoridation's debilitating effects were correct.[8]

Case Studies of Communities
and Content

About 40 percent of the articles fell into this group. This category included both case studies focused on programs in particular communities and general discussion of program content, including programs for teacher education. The case studies were by no means careful analyses of community conflict, and in all cases the articles assumed that sex education was a good thing.

Strategies of Adoption

Ten percent of the articles dealt with how to adopt sex education without arousing community opposition. This category also indicates the stress on need generation. These articles focused on implementing the program. There was less exhortation in these articles, but there was an assumption that sex education was something the reader wanted. The authors usually prescribed careful selection and training of teachers, preparation of parents, and involvement of the community in program planning.

Some proponents argued that since sex education occurred in classrooms in most schools prior to the existence of any formal program, it was educationally sound, completely honest, and politically astute to claim that the programs were not really new. Thus, the proper strategy was to emphasize that sex education was really being expanded and improved rather than initiated. "The public is less afraid of expanding than of innovating and has more confidence in the judgement of school officials who have forged ahead than of those who, because of fear or indifference, have neglected an important aspect of education."[9]

The following publication of the National School Public Relations Association illustrated the content and tone of this literature. Though this piece was not included in the content analysis because it is not actually an article in a journal, it is a good example of the hortatory need-generating strategy. It defends the need for school sex education in two ways. First, it stresses the severe degree of moral change in society:

From the romantic June-moon-spoon era of 1900, the sexual attitudes of America's young seem to have evolved into the swinging "come-on-baby-light-my-fire" bravado of the late 60's—a development that has adults all shook up and young people considerably confused.[10]

Next, it argues that these moral developments create an educational vacuum that schools must fill. The argument for teaching sex education is based on the by now familiar assertion that parents and churches do not do the job.

Parents today are more afraid not to educate their own offspring as to "right" and healthy attitudes in a rapidly changing society.
   But they are hindered by their own ambivalent and emotional feelings about sex. . . . And they frequently don't know the right words! . . .
   If many parents feel helpless in this area, what about the church . . . ?
   Most religious educators say that it is only recently that the church has begun

to overcome its own former reluctance to deal openly with sexual matters, and while it can perform important supportive functions, the church has too limited contact with the children to make an impact.[11]

The third and fourth sections of the report tell the local administrator how to get the program. These two sections attempt to explain to the school administrator what sex education is, in general terms, and present methods for its implementation. The rest of the pamphlet is concerned mainly with curriculum suggestions grouped by grade level. Still, the emphasis is on the need for sex education. Roughly 40 percent of the content is devoted to a hortatory discussion of the reasons for adopting the program. Only about 30 percent concerns the resources and manpower needed for program implementation.

The school district data developed for this book also clearly demonstrate that schoolmen and their close allies initiated these programs. In brief, in 49 percent of the districts programs were initiated by school officials, while 32 percent were initiated by the closely allied parent-teacher organization, the Parent Teacher Association. Groups outside the schools' traditional sphere of influence rank a very poor third as initial suggestors of this program; as Table 4-2 shows, citizen groups were disproportionately associated with sex program opponents. The most striking finding is that 59 percent of the opponents, but only 17 percent of the proponents, were "citizens or citizen groups." This rather nebulous category included groups that school superintendents were less able to identify as on-going interest groups with specific functions. Proponents are primarily parents, students, and parent-teacher groups.

As expected, once the issue was raised by school officials, its proponents were likely to be a coalition of diverse groups, most either sharing regular access to the educational policy process or considered by the policy-makers as a responsible source of information. They were, in short, likely to be part of the educational policy-makers' regular clientele. On the other hand, opponents were

Table 4-2
Sources of Opposition and Support for Family Life/Sex Education

Community Agent	Percent of Opponents	Percent of Proponents
Citizen or Citizen Groups	59	17
Ministers or Religious Groups	18	22
Medical or Health Organizations	11	16
PTA, PTO, "Parents," or Students	7	30
Teachers, Administration or Board	5	10
"Public Officials"	–	4
	$N = 44$	$N = 117$

far more likely to be citizen groups not so considered by our schoolmen respondents (Table 4-3). School officials were not only the most likely to propose sex education; they were also most likely to take unequivocally favorable positions upon first consideration. Few chose other options; only 17 percent of the school boards and 6 percent of the school superintendents took no stand, and only one-fifth of either urged further study. Rather, the large majority of each of these groups supported sex education, and only 2 percent of the school boards and 3 percent of the school superintendents opposed. In contrast, *none* of the citizen groups urged further study, only 4 percent were even equivocal enough to take no stand during the early stages, while almost half opposed adoption.

School Superintendent Professionalization

If professionalization is an important factor leading to the consideration and possible adoption of sex education programs, then districts whose superintendents have relatively advanced professional credentials should have been more likely to consider the programs. They should be more responsive to the generation of need.

The school superintendents were asked whether they held a doctorate, how many different districts they had been employed in, and whether they had ever been the superintendent in another district. Each of these questions provides some basis for assessing the professionalization of the superintendent.[12] Whether or not the administrator had a doctorate is the most important differentiating factor.

Professional training was a factor contributing to consideration of sex education. Sixty-eight percent of the superintendents without doctorates were in districts that had considered these programs, while 81 percent of those with doctorates were in districts that had made such considerations. This is one indication that districts whose superintendents had had more formal exposure to the norms of the profession were more likely to consider adoption.

Table 4-3
Stand of Superintendent, School Board, and Citizens During First Consideration of Family Life/Sex Education

	Superintendent	School Board	"Citizens"
Favored	72%	61%	48%
Took No Stand	6	17	4
Urged Further Study	19	20	0
Opposed	3	2	48
	N = 351	356	29

Cosmopolitanism may be another indicator, though we must be careful in making any conclusions about this measure, because it may be a part of professionalization or it may exert an independent effect. Superintendents who held doctorates are generally more likely than other superintendents to have more cosmopolitan sorts of backgrounds. For example, superintendents with doctorates were significantly more likely than the other such administrators to have been a superintendent in at least one other district before the present one (39 percent of those without doctorates compared to 63 percent of those with doctorates). In addition, the average number of school districts in which they had worked throughout their educational careers was significantly greater than that of those who did not have doctorates. The average number of districts in which superintendents had been employed was 3.7. Sixty-four percent of the superintendents with doctorates, but only 38 percent without doctorates, were above this average. But a superintendent may well have numerous advanced degrees and still be local in his orientation. The district that employs him may then be localistic as well.

One other attribute of cosmopolitanism, and also of professionalization, is job mobility. A cosmopolitan school superintendent does not think of himself as superintendent of schools in District XYZ as much as he considers himself as a superintendent of schools, employed for the moment by District XYZ. He may become a superintendent in another district some day, and he may have been superintendent in another district before moving to his present one. He defines his career in terms of success in his profession rather than in terms of success in just his local district. He is mobile within his profession rather than within his district.

The sort of mobility we are concerned with is as much subjective as objective, but for our purposes, we rely on an indirect, objective, and quantifiable measure. A superintendent is defined as cosmopolitan if he was employed in another district immediately before assuming his present position and/or if he had held the superintendency in at least one other district. We assume that by choosing to go outside its own ranks for a superintendent, the district accepted a limited set of professional norms. This is especially important, since we wish to make statements about the district on the basis of data pertaining only to the superintendent.

Districts with more cosmopolitan superintendents were more likely to have considered sex education programs. However, the differences are not as large as those found when we considered educational backgrounds. Seventy-nine percent of the superintendents with cosmopolitan attributes (and 70 percent without them) reported that their present district had considered sex education. Cosmopolitanism alone does not have a great impact upon whether or not a school district considered sex education. This raises the question of what happens when cosmopolitanism and professionalism are combined. Each should have an independent impact upon whether or not a school district considers adding a planned sex education program to its curriculum, and, when combined, should reinforce each other. That is, districts whose superintendents have both professional and cosmopolitan attributes should be more likely to consider sex education than districts whose superintendents have only one of them.

Table 4-4 confirms this hypothesis: districts whose superintendents are cosmopolitan professionals are most likely to have considered sex education. Districts with noncosmopolitan and nonprofessional superintendents are least likely to have considered sex education. Districts whose superintendents have either been exposed to professional socialization or have the attributes of cosmopolitanism, but not both, fall between the two extremes.

Table 4-4 also shows that the effect of a combination of cosmopolitanism and professionalism is significantly stronger than the operation of either attribute alone. In fact, the proportion of districts considering sex education is not significantly different when districts with neither cosmopolitan nor professional superintendents are compared to districts with either cosmopolitan or professional superintendents alone. On the other hand, the proportion of districts considering sex education is significantly different when the districts whose superintendents have either cosmopolitan or professional attributes, but not both, are compared to districts whose superintendents possess both attributes of professionalism and cosmopolitanism.

General Innovativeness

If generally innovative districts have at least considered sex education, then we have support for the hypothesis that a general orientation toward innovation spills over into consideration of sex education.

We asked the superintendent to report whether or not the district had tried each of the following innovations:

1. language labs,
2. full-year plan

Table 4-4
Superintendent Professionalism and Consideration of Sex Education

Has District Ever Considered Sex Education	Professional Attributes of Superintendent			
	Neither Cosmopolitan Nor Doctorate	Cosmopolitan	Doctorate	Cosmopolitan and Doctorate
Has Considered it	67%	72%	75%	83%
Has NOT Considered it	33	28	25	17
	N = 87	95	69	178

3. flexible or modular scheduling
4. open classrooms
5. team teaching
6. courses emphasizing "social science" instead of "social studies"

The list is certainly not complete; for example, a number of districts are experimenting with no-grade systems. And some of the programs, such as language labs and team teaching, have been used for a number of years in many school districts. However, the list provides a cross-section of fairly recent additions to, or changes in, public school programs. (The average year of adoption for all of the programs was 1963.) Only two of those innovations listed had been tried by even a majority of the districts for which data are available; 92 percent have tried language labs and 90 percent team teaching. At the other extreme, only about 5 percent of the superintendents reported that their districts had tried a full-year plan.

We constructed an "innovation index" by counting the number of specific innovations tried by the district. This index varies from 0 to 6, and the mean is 3.3 innovations. This mean was used to dichotomize innovativeness into two groups. Districts with three or fewer items will be referred to as "low innovators," while districts reporting more than three items will be referred to as "high innovators."

Low innovators are indeed less likely than high innovators to have considered sex education. Sixty-nine percent of the low innovators considered sex education, but 86 percent of the highly innovative districts did so.

It is also important to consider whether the time when sex education was considered is correlated with speed in considering other educational innovations.[13] A "speed of innovation" score was computed on the basis of the exact year that innovations were tried by each district. (The index was computed by totaling the number of innovations a district had tried and then the year in which each was tried. Thus, if a district had tried only one of the innovations, the "mean" would be the year in which that one innovation was first tried.) The superintendents who said that their districts had considered sex education were also asked to report the year in which it was first considered. If general innovativeness is related to a district's consideration of sex education, then those districts that try educational innovations early should also introduce sex education early.

Table 4-5 provides data for this proposition, and again they are positive. There is a consistent and positive relationship between speed of innovation and the year in which sex education was first considered. Districts that were "faster" innovators generally tended to consider sex education sooner than districts that were slower to innovate in other areas.

Table 4-5
Comparison of Relative Speeds of Other Innovations

Year Sex Education Was First Considered	Speed of Other Innovation			
	1950-62	1963-64	1955-65	1967-70
1950-63	39%	25%	27%	13%
1964-66	25	37	20	28
1967	11	20	25	22
1968-70	25	18	27	37
	N = 80	73	88	67

Conclusion

In many ways, school sex education programs followed what would seem to be a common pattern of curricular innovation. One might expect that, concomitantly, the pattern of actually adopting these programs followed the public relations model. Utilizing this model, the professional would define the extent and mode of citizen participation by asking: "How can we get them to accept our position?" "How do we limit the influence of those ignorant troublemakers?" But in Chapter 3 we pointed out that even though educational conflict is far from endemic, intense, unpredictable conflict can arise. We argued that schoolmen certainly entertain such considerations. In the following chapter we continue the investigation of the paradoxes of educational policy making by looking at the ways schoolmen attempt to manage discontent. In Chapter 6 we shall argue that general innovativeness is an especially important factor in explaining the tension between sex education innovation and community conflict.

5

Sex Education Policy Making and the Failure of the Opposition

Since we are concerned here with opposition levels and with policy content, we must introduce certain indicators of these variables that allow us to compare many school districts. To measure opposition, we used an opposition scale that assigned a score of "zero" (no opposition) if the superintendent reported that there was little or no opposition *and* if he reported that the opposition distributed *no* literature. A district was given a score of "one" (some opposition) if the superintendent reported *either* that there was some or a great deal of opposition or that the opposition distributed literature. A district scored "two" (much opposition) if both these phenomena were present. For the following analysis, we generally combined the first two categories, because the data showed little explanatory difference between the "some opposition" category and the "no opposition" one.

Comparing policy comprehensiveness proved more difficult because of SEP's diversity, as noted below. Because so many diverse subjects could be included in a sex education program, it is inaccurate to dichotomize school districts simply by the presence or absence of a planned program. On the other hand, if we wish to analyze a large number of districts, some reasonable comparative measures of program content must be used. We chose a middle ground. In the survey, school superintendents were presented with a list of topics and asked to identify those that were part of their programs; the list (see Table 5-2) had been developed from a review of many such programs. On the basis of these responses, we dichotomized the districts as "high" and "low," depending on whether they offered more or less than the mean number of topics.

There are some rather glaring problems with this measure. It considers neither the grades in which the subjects are taught nor the degree to which the programs are compulsory. (More will be said about the compulsory nature of these programs in Chapter 8.) It also does not consider homosexuality, a topic that acted as a catalyst for some well-publicized conflicts over sex education that have occurred since these data were gathered. It is nonetheless more sensitive to content than is a measure that simply dichotomizes on the basis of whether or not a program exists.

Opposition Failure

There are basically three ways that opponents of SEP might influence program development. They might prevent schoolmen from offering to the public any opportunity to consider these courses. Their behavior would be a form of the law of anticipated reactions; in this case, school policy makers would anticipate such great opposition strength that they would not even attempt to have SEPs considered. Second, schoolmen might introduce programs only to have them defeated by the opposition prior to SEPs initiation. Finally, opposition might modify or eliminate a program that had already been put into effect; this would require the opposition to force or take advantage of reconsideration of the issue.

Though it is difficult to measure the effects of the law of anticipated reaction, Figure 5-1 suggests that the opposition was not successful in preventing the districts from considering the adoption of the courses. Over three-quarters of all the districts in the sample had at least considered these programs at the time of our survey in 1970.

Figure 5-1 also shows that the second pattern of opposition influence is not very apparent. Seldom did the opponents of SEP succeed in defeating programs during the stage of initial consideration. Seventy-six percent of the districts that considered SEPs adopted a program during that consideration. This percentage is particularly impressive when compared to community adoption of water fluoridation. As Crain, Katz, and Rosenthal point out, the controversial nature of fluoridation was apparent not only in the nature of the campaign to get such programs adopted but also in the inability of the cities to adopt it during their initial consideration of that issue. Only 37 percent of the communities considering fluoridation adopted it after the first round of consideration. That is less than half the percentage of school districts adopting sex education programs

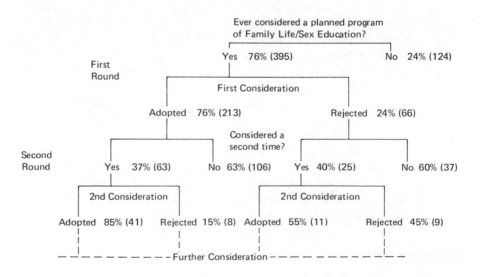

Figure 5-1. Patterns of Consideration of Family Life/Sex Education

after initial consideration. Of those school districts that did not adopt during the first stage, 40 percent reconsidered, and the majority of these adopted some kind of program on second consideration. A slightly lower percentage of the communities in the Crain, Katz, and Rosenthal study reconsidered, and only 17 percent of these adopted at that stage.[1] Other data not reported in Figure 5-1 showed that the level of opposition had no effect on the tendency to adopt on initial consideration.

Thus, even though reconsideration also decreased the likelihood that sex education programs would be adopted, the relationship between reconsideration and rejection was not nearly as high as in the case of fluoridation. Nonetheless, for the opponents this left only the reconsideration stage. Perhaps they were more effective in getting communities to see the errors of their ways and to reconsider. Indeed, many press accounts of sex education conflicts mention some kind of post-SEP incident that triggered the opposition's success. Even then, however, opposition success seemed very limited. In only 5 percent of the entire sample of districts was an existing SEP eliminated; less than 10 percent of the districts that reconsidered made their programs less comprehensive upon second thought, and almost half expanded their programs upon reconsideration. Whatever the indicator of program limitation, we can say that in less than 10 percent of the districts was opposition strong enough to have some direct effect on an already existing program. The inability to mobilize during reconsideration is reflected by the fact that opposition did not greatly increase during reconsideration. Forty-eight percent of the districts that reconsidered reported heavy opposition, as compared to 40 percent of the districts during the initial consideration.

Of more general importance is the relationship between opposition and program content. Districts with much opposition were only slightly less likely to have comprehensive SEPs than were districts with less or no opposition. Fifty-four percent of the former districts had comprehensive SEPs, while 43 percent of the latter did. (Yule's $Q = -.23$) Also, as Table 5-1 shows, even heavy opposition did not seem to make much difference in altering program content; such districts were equally likely to continue and expand existing programs. However, only districts with heavy opposition unilaterally reduced their SEPs upon reconsideration, but these were only 14 percent of all programs in heavy-opposition districts. Surprisingly, districts with some or no opposition were *less* likely to adopt SEP on reconsideration than were those with high opposition. What seems more significant is the similarity between opposition levels in regard to the results of reconsideration. Among the districts reconsidering existing programs, there was virtually no difference in the likelihood that either group would expand their programs.

What explains this failure? If our hypotheses about content alteration and counterinfluence are at all valid, the interaction between schoolman and opponent ought to be explained in terms of such relationships. Along these lines,

Table 5-1
Result of Reconsideration and Level of Opposition

Result of Second Consideration	Opposition Level	
	None or Some	Much
Program Begun	17%	11%
Program Not Begun	16	9
Continued as Was	22	22
Expanded	26	25
Contracted	–	14
Some Expansion, Some Contraction	20	18
N	(46)	(44)

we shall consider the opposition's failure by the ability of schoolman to blunt opposition by altering content.

Content Alteration

Public policies vary in the degree that they can be altered by their advocates without destroying program integrity. Thus, we would expect that the more amenable a policy is to what we might call nondestructive content alteration, the more policy-makers are able to manage discontent by such modification. SEPs are extraordinarily flexible. They can vary according to the school class level at which they begin, the subject matter, the discipline through which the subject is introduced, and the degree that the course is required.

The importance of such flexibility to the policy process is reflected in the fact that the ten items we used to measure the comprehensiveness of SEPs form a Guttman scale as seen in Table 5-2. The high coefficient of reproducibility in Table 5-2 indicates unidimensionality in school policy makers' perceptions of opposition levels. Putting it another way, a topic was not likely to be included unless all of the more common topics were also taught. The high degree of unidimensionality indicates that these topics are likely adopted in the sequence shown. This flexibility was an important factor in preventing the opposition from defeating a program during initial consideration. Schoolmen were able to implement programs gradually. They could argue that they had "always" had some sex education in their district's curriculum, whether in health, biology, family living, or literature courses. In this way, community anxieties were allayed because, schoolmen argued, curricular readjustments rather than basic innovations were taking place. Our survey asked about "planned programs," a phrase that suggests some specific mobilization of resources and special concern.

Table 5-2
Frequency of Topics Taught in Sex Education Programs

Topic	Percent of Districts Offering Topic
Planned Parenthood	39
Prostitution	41
Masturbation	51
Seminal Emissions	55
Ethical Standards	57
Dating, Petting, Necking	62
Anatomy of Genital Organs	63
Venereal Diseases	66
Changes in Adolescence	67
Human Reproduction	68

Coefficient of Reproducibility = .92
Minimum Marginal Reproducibility = .61
Coefficient of Scalability = .79

Nonetheless, the more subtle and gradual content alterations noted above undoubtedly took place within the confines of such planning. As Chapter 4 showed, professional proponents of SEPs saw this as an important strategy for gaining adoption.

There is a more subtle way that this kind of content alteration affects the opposition's abilities to cancel an already existing program. Program flexibility made it more likely that policies could be developed at the low level of visibility that generally accompanies curricular change. The ability to tinker with programs, to experiment with their contents, made it more likely that bureaucratization of conflict would occur. Such bureaucratization tends to remove an issue from conflict-laden situations, and subsequently, when the heat dies down, the bureaucracies make policy. Such situations, in short, exacerbate the opposition's problem of maintaining surveillance over the policy process.

Opposition and Counterinfluence

Despite SEP flexibility, the potential for conflict and, thus, the dilemma between innovation and conflict were still apparent. There are two indications of this. First, the level of opposition was rather high and increased slightly when the issue was reconsidered. During initial consideration, 40 percent of the districts encountered much opposition to SEPs, while only 27 percent had no opposition at all. Almost half of the reconsidered districts encountered much opposition, but only 20 percent experienced no opposition during reconsideration.

Second, schoolmen seemed to see sex education as an especially controversial issue that required special sensitivity to opposition. Table 5-3 shows that they claimed that this program's policy making required a special concern for the views of the parents in their districts. Seventy-seven percent of the schoolmen believed that they "should have final say" on curricular matters in general, but more (81 percent) were willing to grant the citizen's right to consult on such matters. Responses to sex education, however, were quite different. Even more schoolmen (91 percent) believed that parents should be consulted on SEP matters, and 72 percent of the schoolmen believed that professionals should *not* have the final say on SEP issues. Since the questionnaire was almost entirely about sex education, it is biased toward viewing SEP as a special issue. Still, the difference in attitudes about others' participation in this issue is quite dramatic. Given the tension between innovation and conflict, we would expect that this awareness of the "special" qualities of sex education would make schoolmen especially sensitive to the adoption of mechanisms that take into account levels of opposition if not the substance of the opponents' demands.

Opposition was high, but its direct effect on program adoption seemed minimal. Schoolmen seemed more willing to allow citizen participation in SEP development. Yet, on the surface, such participation, if it existed, did not seem to make much difference in the likelihood of a program's adoption. All of these combine to describe a policy process indicating counterinfluence as well as content alteration. The discussion that follows shows this is indeed the case. Forms of counterinfluence were rather closely correlated with opposition levels and, to a lesser extent, with SEP comprehensiveness. Again, we shall use the types of policy-making mechanisms as indicators of variations in the counterinfluence process.

In Chapter 3 we hypothesized that opposition to SEP is directly related to the amenability of a chosen form of policy making to citizen involvement. The relationship between discontent management and opposition worked two ways. First, mechanisms may have been chosen in response to the degree of opposition, and second, opposition may have been affected by the mechanism authorities chose to use. The data here cannot clearly establish which one is more important, but there is evidence that both patterns occurred.

Table 5-4 shows that during the initial consideration the hypothesized relationship between mechanisms and opposition levels existed. With the exception of lay-person committees, the more the initially used policy-making forum was oriented to mass participation, the greater the degree of opposition to the programs. Sixty-five percent of the districts using public meetings during the first consideration had a high level of opposition. In comparison, 46 percent of the districts using "mixed" committees (those composed of both professionals

Table 5-3
School Superintendent Attitudes About Participation in Educational Policy Making

	Educators should consult parents about curricular matters	Educators should have final say on curricular matters	Educators should consult parents about courses in family life/sex education	Educators should have final say about family life/sex education courses
Agree	81%	77%	91%	28%
Disagree	19	23	9	72
Total	100	100	100	100
(N)	(508)	(499)	(510)	(489)

Table 5-4
Level of Opposition and Policy-Making Mechanisms Used in SEP Considerations

Policy-Making Mechanisms	Level of Opposition		
	Much	None or Some	(*N*)
Public Meeting			
First Consideration	65%	35	(31)
Second Consideration	80	20	(10)
Committee Only of Lay Persons			
First Consideration	15	85	(7)
Second Consideration	20	80	(10)
"Mixed" Committee[a]			
First Consideration	46	54	(46)
Second Consideration	30	70	(10)
Committee of School Professionals/School Bd.			
First Consideration	36	64	(56)
Second Consideration	60	40	(47)
Unilateral Policy Making			
First Consideration	28	72	(46)
Second Consideration[b]			

[a]"Mixed" = Committee composed of both lay persons and school professionals
[b]Data unavailable
Kendall's tau for first consideration = .239

and lay persons), 36 percent of those using committees with no lay persons, and only 28 percent in districts using neither committees nor public meetings (unilateral policy making) had opposition of this intensity.

Table 5-4 also shows that the relationship between mass participation and opposition is less clear for those districts reconsidering the issue. Though public meetings continued to be associated with the greatest opposition (80 percent), the three committee mechanisms followed no expected pattern. Opposition was highest among districts that used professional/school board committees during reconsideration. There is little difference between the other two committee forms. We will subsequently discuss the significance of the different patterns during this stage.

Table 5-5 shows this relationship in another way. It compares districts with heavy opposition to those with less or no opposition. The more extreme a mechanism was, *either* in its amenability *or* lack of amenability to lay person participation, the greater the difference in the frequency between the use by

Table 5-5
Policy-Making Mechanisms and Level of Opposition—First Consideration

Mechanisms:	Level of Opposition		Percentage Differences
	None or Some	Much	
Public Meeting	8%	19%	+11
Committees of Lay Persons Only	4	1	−3
"Mixed" Committee	44	51	+7
Committee of Professionals/School Board	22	17	−5
Unilateral Policy Making	22	12	−10
(N)	(147)	(107)	

low/no-opposition and higher-opposition districts. The direction of those differences in Table 5-5 is also correct. Public meetings and unilateral policy making show the largest differences. The differences become smaller for the three forms of committees. Again, the lay-person committee is the exception. We expected the districts with heavy opposition would have used this structure with much greater frequency than the other districts did. In fact, other districts used it more frequently.

The relationship between counterinfluence and opposition is even more evident in Table 5-6, where we look at important combinations of policy-making mechanisms that were used. Three findings are significant. Regardless of whether or not they also used public meetings, those districts that used committees had less opposition than those few using only public meetings. Districts that used public meetings and mixed professional/school board committees were quite likely to have high levels of opposition (over 70 percent of these districts), but this is slightly *lower* than the percentage of high-opposition cases in districts using *only* public meetings during at least one consideration. Second, all committee-users were more likely to have intense opposition than were those using unilateral policy making. Third, within both the professional/school board and mixed committee groups, those that also used public meetings were far more likely to have heavy opposition (Yule's Q for mixed committees = .42; Yule's Q for professional committeess = .64). Taken together, these findings reveal that the opposition was indeed heaviest where the district used a form amenable to its development and where the district did not also use a mechanism conducive to co-optation. But public meetings were also important even within districts using less mass-oriented and perhaps more co-optative mechanisms of discontent management. In short, the schoolmen's distrust of public meetings appears well founded, if we consider only opposition levels. However, we must go beyond this consideration.

In order to discover how this relationship between opposition and policy-

Table 5-6

Committees of Public Meetings and Opposition Level—Both Considerations Combined

Committee:	Was Public Meeting Also Used?	Opposition Level		
		Much	Some or None	(N)
Lay Persons Only	Yes	50%	50%	(4)
	No	13	87	(15)
Mixed	Yes	72	28	(22)
	No	31	69	(110)
Professionals/School Board	Yes	71	29	(81)
	No	39	61	(14)
Public Meeting[a]		78%	22%	(11)
Unilateral[b]		30	70	(68)

[a]These districts used only a public meeting during at least one consideration.
[b]These districts used unilateral policy making during at least one consideration.

making mechanism was indicative of typical opposition failure, it is necessary to consider the role of predictability in the policy process, just as we considered it in regard to content alteration. Since SEP opponents tended to come from political outgroups, or at least from those not regularly participating in the policy process, the opponents clearly were compelled to upset the business-as-usual policy process. Schoolmen succeeded in making the policies by using business-as-usual methods. If opposition was heavy—as it frequently was—then policy-making forums used to counterinfluence heavy opposition were typically used. This predictability decreases the likelihood that a schoolman will introduce a policy that is so unexpectedly controversial that its entire existence, as well as his professional integrity, is threatened.

Though opponents were not usually very successful during the reconsideration, our data suggest that this stage was more of a problem for some schoolmen, because predictability was more difficult at that stage. Some did not correctly predict the functions of a reconsideration and thus underestimated the opposition's intensity. The importance of predictability is underscored if we look more closely at the reconsideration stage, which involved two very different processes. First, it reflected an attempt to strengthen already existing programs. In this case the reconsideration had a certain business-as-usual aura about it. Schoolmen assumed that the program was basically sound and secure. Those districts attempting to strengthen an existing program were likely to use a form of policy making that was more useful for implementing already existing curricular programs for which there seemed little objection. In such cases, less mass-oriented mechanisms were likely to be used.

On the other hand, reconsideration offered an opportunity for the opposition to question the program's basic existence. We have already suggested that opponents were seldom successful, but our data suggest that occasionally schoolmen did miscalculate. Misunderstanding the ways others would view the purpose of reconsideration, they chose policy-making mechanisms that were not very mass-oriented or public. These mechanisms were vulnerable to charges of elitism or steamrolling in cases where the schoolmen assumed that reconsideration was for the purpose of easy gradual expansion but where the opposition thought otherwise. The surprisingly high level of opposition accompanying the use of a professional/school board committee during reconsideration (Table 5-4) suggests that schoolmen made this kind of tactical error regarding their choice of policy-making mechanisms for reconsideration. Compared to all other districts, those using these committees showed the greatest increase in opposition between first and second considerations. Only 36 percent of districts using this mechanism initially had heavy opposition, while 60 percent experienced such opposition upon reconsideration (Yule's $Q = -.42$).

What, if any, are the direct policy implications of this relationship between forum and opposition levels? In Chapter 3 we hypothesized that the methods of discontent management, especially counterinfluence, would be related not merely to the levels of opposition but also to the kind of policy that results. The less amenable a policy-making mechanism is to citizen participation, the more comprehensive is the policy that results. In fact, the hypothesized relationship between mechanisms and process is not quite so clear cut for either consideration (Table 5-7). Contrary to the hypothesis, during the first consideration, districts using lay-person committees were less likely to have comprehensive programs than were those that used the more mass-oriented public meetings. There is little difference between the two other committees or between either of these two committees and unilateral policy-making districts. The same is generally true of the second consideration also. The only difference is that, during the reconsideration, districts using only public meetings were least likely to have comprehensive SEPs. Only lay committees showed an important difference between considerations (Yule's $Q = -.51$). Table 5-8 shows that there is a similar pattern when we consider combination of policy-making mechanisms.

Though the relationship between content and these mechanisms is again less clear than the relationship between opposition levels and mechanisms (compare Table 5-6), there is still some evidence that the use of public meetings and lack of co-optative mechanisms affected program content. If we do not consider the anomalous lay-person committees, we find in Table 5-8 that those districts that held only public meetings during at least one consideration and those that used mixed committees *and* public meetings were least likely to have comprehensive programs. Districts using no public meetings were most likely to have relatively highly comprehensive programs.

If we do not consider districts using lay-person committees and rank-order

Table 5-7
Policy-Making Mechanisms and SEP Comprehensiveness

| | | Comprehensiveness Consideration: | | |
		Low	High	(*N*)
Public Meetings Only	First	56%	44%	(7)
	Second	67	33	(3)
Lay-Person Committee	First	73	27	(11)
	Second	46	54	(13)
Mixed Committee	First	44	56	(189)
	Second	50	50	(34)
Professional/School Board	First	49	51	(70)
	Second	50	50	(40)
Unilateral	First	37	63	(93)
	Second	38	62	(29)

Kendall's Tau   First consideration = .036
Kendall's Tau   Second consideration = .135

Table 5-8
Committees, Public Meetings, and SEP Comprehensiveness—Both Considerations Combined

| Committee Mechanism | Was Public Meeting Also Used? | SEP Comprehensiveness | | |
		Low	High	(*N*)
Lay Person	Yes	50%	50%	(2)
	No	69	31	(16)
Mixed	Yes	62	38	(29)
	No	43	57	(193)
Professional	Yes	53	47	(17)
	No	48	52	(93)
Public Meeting[a]		60%	40%	(10)
Unilateral[b]		38	62	(122)

[a]Districts that used only public meetings during at least one consideration
[b]Districts that used unilateral policy making during at least one consideration

the policy-making mechanisms, the predicted over-all relationship between content and forum is more apparent (Table 5-9). The rank order correlation is +0.6. The strength of this correlation suggests that, while the relationship between mechanism and content may not be as strong as the relationship between mechanism and opposition, they both follow similar and relatively

Table 5-9
Rank-Order Correlations Between Opposition and SEP Comprehensiveness

Rank of Table 5-5 Mechanisms from Low to High Opposition	Rank of Table 5-7 Mechanisms from Low to High Program Content
1. Unilateral Policy Making	1. Unilateral Policy Making
2. Mixed Committees with No Public Meeting	2. Mixed Committees with No Public Meeting
3. Professional/School Committee with No Public Meeting	3. Professional/School Committee with No Public Meeting
4. Professional/School Committee with Public Meeting	4. Professional/School Committee with Public Meeting
5. Mixed Committee with Public Meeting	*5. Public Meetings Only
6. Public Meetings Only	*6. Mixed Committee with Public Meeting
$r = .6$	* = Virtual Tie

predictable patterns. In both cases, professional/school committees did not fare as well as we originally anticipated, but we repeat that this lack of success may be due to tactical errors in the use of this committee during reconsideration. Ultimately, predictability worked to limit the opponents' effectiveness in modifying the program.

**Conclusion: Conflict Mitigation,
Opposition Failure, and the
Availability of Resources**

In this chapter we have shown that the hypothesized relationships between policy-making mechanisms and opposition levels do exist as do the relationships between these mechanisms and program content. We have also shown that this pattern tends to work to the disadvantage of the opposition. This is not to say that the opponents of SEP typically had no influence. The very flexibility of the SEP policy process meant that the wise schoolman could easily adjust his program to meet this opposition, if he thought such an adjustment was necessary. But we must remember that in the eyes of many of the opponents this is not much of a victory, because it allowed SEPs to exist, perhaps even in a form that required opponents' children to take the courses. Moreover, this settlement did not significantly question the professional authority of the school policy maker.

The obstacles that flexibility and predictability place in the way of the opposition's success can be considered in terms of the resource limitations they created or exacerbated.[2] We have already suggested that the flexibility of SEPs creates two kinds of problems for the opposing groups or individuals. First, it makes it easier to introduce programs gradually without much visibility. Second, it makes it easier for bureaucracies to modify the programs. Because of the SEPs' amenability to content alteration, the programs could be constantly reviewed and readjusted by those who develop curriculum. This flexibility increased the likelihood that conflict could be bureaucratized. Thus, opponents had to try to survey a pattern of decisions that traditionally took place well beneath the surface. This required access and continuous commitment to the issue even after it was no longer salient. Indeed, it involved keeping it visible. Even the most intense and militant community groups generally lacked the resources to do so. In this way, content alteration and form of discontent management dovetail.

The opponents' inability to control the salience of an issue seemed evident in another way. Literature favoring the SEPs was seldom distributed in districts where there was no opposition literature. Over 75 percent of the districts where proponent literature appeared also had opposition literature. Absence of time-series data preclude direct evidence that proponent literature was distributed only as a response to opposition, but this would follow from the fact that the impetus for SEPs typically did not come from citizens' groups. On the surface, it might appear that this pattern of distribution reflects the high initiative of the opposition; by moving the question from inside the administration to a more public arena, the opponents tried to force the policy-makers' hands. But the more significant point is that the opposition probably had to expend resources to get the issue considered outside the realm of the usual educational policy process. Again, an important obstacle was the opponents' typical lack of access to the kinds of communication resources that seemed necessary to get their definition of the situation accepted by either majority.

The proponents generally were supported by those groups and individuals likely to control the forms of news communication that reached the populace most easily. The lack of proponent literature thus reflects not as much a lack of initiative as a degree of strength. Since making SEP development visible would seem to be disadvantageous for the typical policy-making process, it is not surprising that, unless pressed, proponents did not expend resources to increase counterproductive activity. Of course, this passivity occasionally backfired, and opponents got the initiative that they needed to transcend business as usual, but this opponent success is atypical.

To make this conclusion clearer, let us briefly reconsider the comparison we have made between SEP and fluoridation. The differences between the ease with which SEP and fluoridation became a reality can be attributed less to differences in the makeup of the participants than in the policy mechanisms at work. Educational policy making is traditionally more top-down and public-relations-oriented than is the process used by fluoridation decision-makers. Also, the either/or nature of fluoridation forced the policy-makers' hands. Finally, there was no way that fluoridation could be adopted solely within the barely visible confines of a community bureaucracy. All of this made it more difficult to prevent fluoridation from becoming a public issue, and easier for opponents to disrupt, and keep informed about, the process. In short, the presence of partisans who do not accept the norms of policy making is not enough to guarantee that public policy will be affected, even on issues with a potential for serious moral conflict. What also must be present are a setting and structure that limit the policy-makers' ability to make changes and to limit conflict. Putting all this another way, opponents have to expend resources not only to *keep* school sex education an issue but also to *make it one in the first place*. Combining this with the fact that schoolmen seemed to be rather good discontent managers, we can see that opposition to this form of school policy making faced pretty severe obstacles at each stage of SEP consideration.

This conclusion may seem contrary to the general discussions of SEP that appear in the mass media. Not surprisingly, news media are far more likely to emphasize the conflict and the success of the opposition because of media interest in newsworthy cases. Thus, they describe situations that approach the ideal politico-moral conflict discussed in Chapter 1. We do not deny the importance of these exceptional cases, but in most cases the opposition was blunted in its attempt to convince others of the moral seriousness of the issue. For the most part, this was true even when the opponents were able to use what on the surface appeared to be a forum very amenable to their influence.

6   **Innovativeness Reconsidered**

This chapter provides a bridge between the preceding chapter, which focuses on schoolmen's conflict containment strategies, and Chapter 7, which presents case studies of two communities in which extensive conflict over sex education occurred. Here we consider two questions related to bureaucratization, participation, and the development of SEPs. First, what relatively long-term structural and cultural conditions affect the development of SEP? Second, can we offer more details about the *process* that interrelates innovation and political conflict?

Social analysts, some of whom we have already relied on in this work, have been increasingly concerned with the first question. Their analysis of the long-term determinants of policy have included investigation of "both continuing or recurring and patterned situations and relatively unchanging elements of the society and polity," as well as "value commitments of groups within the community as a whole, expressed through laws and policies."[1] More specifically, these include the forms of government, racial and religious and class distributions, and the economic base of the community. Such studies have sought to transcend the participants' motivations and strategies by placing a specific decision or issue in a broader social and political context.

Despite the importance of this approach, we can use it only to a limited degree in the present study, given our focus on school districts. Little relevant school district data are available. There is nothing comparable to the *Municipal Year Book* or the reports of the Bureau of Census, each of which furnishes virtually all of the information needed to construct indicators of communities' enduring sociopolitical characteristics. We considered generating such data ourselves by asking schoolmen or others in the districts to furnish such information in our questionnaires. We discovered, however, that schoolmen simply do not have such information easily available. They furnished us with some information, e.g., the method of school board selection and financial resources, but our analyses of these showed that they alone had limited value in helping us understand the policy process. We also tried to superimpose school districts on community boundaries to see if, with some adjustments, we could use the community data. This strategy was not fruitful, because the fit was too irregular and, thus, too many questionable assumptions had to be made.

Rather than eliminate this type of approach entirely, we chose to focus on the data that (with some inferences, which we shall defend) can be used as indicators of some of these enduring cultural and structural characteristics. These data refer to the *general innovativeness* of the school district, which, we shall argue, is an important indicator of enduring patterns of bureaucratization and participation. In Chapter 4 we showed that districts that were generally more innovative on educational matters were more likely to have SEPs. Now we shall consider innovation in a structural sense. We are not concerned with the individual characteristics of the innovators.

This perspective helps gain insight into a basic anomaly regarding opposition and innovation: innovativeness and opposition to sex education go together. We saw this in earlier discussions, and data often show this to be the case. About half (49 percent) of the highly innovative districts had heavy opposition on the SEP issue, while only about 40 percent of the low innovators had that much opposition. Later we shall look at how the opposition affected the comprehensiveness of SEPs in these two groups of districts. For now we merely want to establish the fact that innovative districts had more opposition to begin with.

The anomaly exists only if one expects that districts that were more willing to adopt the SEPs did so because they encountered less opposition. The discussion in Chapter 5, however, suggested that districts with highly comprehensive SEPs were better able to *control* or *manage* discontent. Such districts were not necessarily able to prevent opposition from developing. This anomaly disappears if one can argue that in certain kinds of school districts opposition and innovation go together. We shall argue that political and structural characteristics exist in such districts which *both* encourage participation *and* facilitate the mobilization of resources necessary for innovation.

To solve this riddle we must first elaborate upon the structures and processes reflected in a school district's ability to innovate. Next we shall look at sex education policy making in these terms. Finally, we shall attempt to make the linkage between innovation and conflict more explicit and thus provide a more complete answer to the second question we raised in the introduction to this chapter, the answer to which requires an understanding of the *process* relating innovativeness and conflict management.

The Structure and Process of Innovation

We assume that general innovativeness is an indicator of a high level of bureaucratization. A political unit's ability to innovate depends to a great extent on the preexistence of organizations and institutions that can rapidly mobilize in response to pressure for change, whether that change is initiated within or outside of the organization. Innovative districts have learned how to mobilize for change and have the preexisting resources to do so. This ability to mobilize transcends any single policy area, and it is supported by the political culture and structures of the community. We find that community policy making studies helps to explain why the same communities tend to be innovative in very disparate policy areas. For example, cities that had already adopted an urban renewal program were more likely to fluoridate their water early on.[2] There is a similar relationship between poverty programs and low-rent housing policies.[3]

Such communities are not simply best able to mobilize their resources to consider new ideas. They are also best able to handle opposition when it impinges upon the policy process. These communities have high levels of participation in addition to high levels of bureaucratization. But the existence of complex bureaucracies and high levels of participation in policy making do not necessarily work at cross purposes. Alford describes these highly bureaucratic and highly participatory communities as "more modern" and "more mobilizable."

A highly bureaucratized, participatory community should be better able and ready to act in certain ways than less bureaucratic and participatory communities. Such a prediction is in line with the literature on political development and modernization, which explicitly holds that a more modern community is more mobilized, in the sense that its decision-making machinery is well developed and there is greater capacity both for organizing citizen preferences into effective political demands and for processing demands into outputs of decisions and policies.[4]

These communities are

probably full of conflict because of the contradiction between the desires of officials to pursue the common interests of the [community] members and the desire of the [community] members to check official performance continuously against the freely chosen goals which justify the actions of those officials.[5]

This does not mean that conflict works to the advantage of the partisans. As Alford's use of the word *processing* suggests, it is not simply that policy-makers have to be more willing to alter their own preferences in response to discontent in more mobilizable communities. Rather, they develop a more complete and sophisticated range of policy-making techniques to handle the tension between bureaucracy and participation by countering the influence of community members. Bureaucracies develop as specialized institutions in part to respond to high levels of political participation. Though in some ways this appears to make policy making more decentralized and more responsive to special interests, this responsiveness alone tells only a small part of the story. Bureaucracies also insulate themselves from intense demands. Their universalism, sense of expertise, and emphasis on general rules lead them to view their constituencies with a certain distrust and to use mechanisms that limit constituency influence.[6]

There are other reasons that bureaucracies act to deflect participation. Since the political culture in highly participative communities encourages participation, it is not surprising that discontented groups feel that taking part in policy making is a legitimate activity. But when such a group demands the *elimination* of a bureaucracy or challenges the basic authority of that bureaucracy, it is also challenging an important community norm. Bureaucracies seek to manage such discontent by claiming the authority to exclude opposition groups from participation. Putting it another way, in the abstract, the participation orientation may encourage those groups that tend to derogate existing policy-making authority, but the bureaucratic orientation in a modern community typically limits the effectiveness of such groups in blunting any demands that challenge the authority of the existing policy process.

In short, the modern community is innovative for three reasons. First, it has specialists and experts who are sensitive and attuned to the needs for innovation. Our earlier discussion of innovation showed this to be the case regarding SEP. Second, the dominant political culture of the community is supportive of the *process* that leads to or facilitates innovation. Third, such communities can take advantage of high levels of participation either by altering the content of policies or by structuring participation in ways that bureaucracies are especially good at doing.

By analogy, we assume that an innovative school district is similarly modern. There are, however, some major differences between our assumptions about school districts and Alford's findings about communities. Alford refers to policy-making activities that cover a wide range of subjects, while we are concerned only with school policy making, and with only one aspect of school policy making at that. Though we assume that modern communities tend to be more innovative on educational matters, we have no data to support this assumption. Still, others, including Alford, have suggested the same analogy.[7] Because we associate mobilization and modernization with innovation, we use these words or combinations of them interchangeably in the following discussion.

Innovation and Discontent Management

The Importance of Committees in Innovative Districts

Again we must be concerned with the policy-making mechanisms that were used to make SEPs. In this context committee usage takes on particular significance. High levels of participation and specialized decision-making structures encourage the use of committees, because on the one hand, this form of policy making is consistent with cultural values stressing official accountability, and on the other hand, committees also allow for structuring this participation. Thus, we would expect that modern, mobilized, highly innovative school districts would use committees more than the low innovators would. Because mixed committees indicate co-optation and because co-optation very nicely handles the bureaucracy-participation tension, we also anticipate that high innovators would be more likely to use mixed committees. These hypotheses are confirmed by our data. Thirty-two percent of the low innovators used no committees during the initial consideration, while only 22 percent of the higher innovators failed to use a committee. During the second consideration, the differences were slightly greater, as 29 percent of the low innovators compared to only 17 percent of the high innovators failed to use some form of committees. During both considerations the innovative districts were more likely to use committees composed of both lay persons and professionals (57 to 45 percent during the first and 13 as compared to 10 percent during the second). These differences remain for the first consideration even if we control for the fact that high innovators used committees more frequently. Using such controls, we find that during the first consideration 66 percent of the low innovators *that used committees* chose the mixed committee, while 74 percent of the high innovators that used committees did so. During the second consideration, these differences disappeared because high innovators relied much more heavily on committees comprised only of professionals or school board members.

Those who failed to use committees, of course, used one of two totally different policy-making mechanisms: public meetings or unilateral policy making. During the first consideration, 17 percent of the low innovators and 13 percent of the mobilized districts held public meetings on the SEP issue. This is not surprising, because a simple model of innovation and discontent management would lead one to believe that the hands of schoolmen in mobilized school districts could not be forced in such a way as to make them hold such meetings.

Far more interesting, however, is the fact that during the all-important first consideration, 26 percent of the low innovators as compared to only 18 percent of the high innovators used unilateral policy making. This is another indicator of the strength of the participatory norms in mobilized, innovative districts and the special needs in such districts to cope with the tension between bureaucracy and participation. Concomitantly, it is further evidence to support the previously discussed relationship between modernity and mobilization.

In sum, the two groups of districts mobilized their responses to the SEP issue rather differently. As anticipated, these differences seem best explained by viewing innovation from a structural and cultural perspective that views bureaucratization and participation as processes that remain relatively stable from issue to issue. The response patterns in innovative districts suggest that they acted in ways characteristic of modern, mobilizable political systems with all the tensions between bureaucracy and participation that this mobilization entails.

Sex Education Policy Content in
the Modern School District

Again we must face the ultimate question, "What effect do these differences in patterns of mobilization/innovation have on policy output?" Generally we would expect that innovative districts would not only be more likely to consider and adopt SEPs, but also that these programs would tend to be more comprehensive. Our data support this. Forty percent of the low innovators had highly comprehensive SEPs, while 60 percent of the high innovators had such programs.

But what of the effects of the opposition? Are the preexisting biases toward mobilization strong enough to blunt the effects even of SEP opposition? We shall test the hypothesis that in modern districts opposition levels did not effect the comprehensiveness of SEPs.

Table 6-1 shows that this hypothesis is confirmed. We had expected to find a difference in the comprehensiveness of SEPs according to opposition levels in less modern districts but to find no such difference in the modern districts (represented by scores on the innovativeness scale). In fact, 51 percent of the less innovative districts without opposition had extensive SEPs, whereas only 34 percent of these districts had extensive SEPs when opposition was present. The difference is significant at the .001 level. When we look at the modern districts—those scoring high on the innovative index—a similar trend appears to operate. But the percentages are misleading, since a test of significance shows no difference between the two groups. In fact, the only other comparison (Table 6-1), which is not statistically significant, is that between low innovation-little opposition and high innovation-much opposition. Putting it another way, in highly innovative districts with low opposition, chances were about two-to-one in favor of the adoption of comprehensive SEPs. The odds were about even in both the innovative districts with much opposition and in the noninnovative districts with little or no opposition. The odds were two-to-one against adoption of comprehensive SEPs in less innovative districts where opposition to SEP was rather high. From the standpoint of educational policy makers who desire SEPs, it was still better not to have opposition than to have much opposition in a modern, mobilized, innovative school district. At least it was no worse having low opposition in districts that were not easily mobilizable than it was to have mobilizable districts with much opposition.

Table 6-1
SEP Comprehensiveness Controlling for District Innovativeness and Level of Opposition[a]

Level of Opposition	Innovativeness	
	Low	High
None-Some	51% (85)	66% (64)
Much	34% (38)	54% (60)

[a]Entries are percentages of districts in a cell with comprehensive SEPs. Numbers in parentheses are total cases for the cells.

Nonethcless, a preexisting propensity to mobilize seemed to play some role. High levels of mobilization or opposition had the most deleterious effect in less innovative districts, where only about one-third of the districts that had such opposition developed comprehensive SEPs. While modernization did not guarantee that opposition would be blunted, the lack of modernization increased the likelihood that SEP opponents could alter the content of sex education programs.

More specifically, what made less modernized districts more susceptible to the effects of opposition? One possibility is that opposition was simply less familiar to schoolmen in these districts. In modernized districts, high levels of participation were endemic, while in less innovative districts high levels of participation, particularly in the form of opposition, were more of an aberration. Thus, the issue of familiarity, discussed in Chapters 3 and 5, comes to the fore again. Policy-makers in the less innovative district were less familiar with, and less prepared for, the opposition and consequently were more likcly to choose the inappropriate policy-making mechanism to counter the influence of SEP opponents.

Thorough testing of the relationship among modernization, familiarity, policy-making mechanisms, and program content requires more data on districts' social and political characteristics than we have at our disposal. Nevertheless, we can get some further indication of the linkages by considering the use of unilateral policy making.

Unilateral policy making is an extreme form of policy making; policy-makers would use it only if they believe that opposition is not likely to have serious consequences. From our earlier discussion in this chapter, we already know that modern districts were less likely to use this form of policy making because typically it is not conducive to resolving the tension between bureaucratization and participation that characterized these districts. If schoolmen in modern districts were indeed better able to gauge opposition levels, when they did decide to use this particularly risky mechanism, they should have been more successful. Table 6-2 shows that this was the case.

Table 6-2
SEP Comprehensiveness Controlling for District Innovativeness and the Use of Unilateral Policy Making[a]

Used Unilateral Techniques	Innovativeness	
	Low	High
No	46%(144)	59%(143)
Yes	57% (53)	73% (33)

[a]Entries are percentage of districts in a cell with comprehensive SEPs. Numbers in parentheses are total cases for the cell.

Schoolmen in modern districts did quite well with unilateral policy making the few times it was used. Seventy-three percent of the innovative/modern districts that used unilateral policy making during SEP consideration adopted comprehensive programs. Nothing else in Table 6-2 approaches this number. The odds were about three-to-one that a schoolman guessed correctly when he chose unilateral policy making in a modern district, while the odds were about even if other mechanisms were used or if unilateral policy making was used in less modern districts.

Conclusion

Modernization seems to be an important factor in school district policy making. It creates resources that give educational policy-makers an advantage in calculating the risks involved in policy formation and development. Putting it in terms of the discussion in Chapter 3, modernization helps schoolmen determine with greater sensitivity just how much they must adjust to the activities of their opponents. These advantages hold even (or perhaps especially) when school policy-makers choose mechanisms that seem contrary to a district's political norms.

The manifestations of modernization create such advantages in two ways. First, in a modern district there is a greater number of specialized agencies available to respond to participation by countering its influence. Second, because both high levels of participation and bureaucratization are so much a part of the modern policy process, schoolmen in modern districts have more experience in handling the tensions that result. This skill is manifested in their frequent use of committees. In addition, schoolmen in modern districts have greater skills in determining when the tension does *not* exist, i.e., when the norms favoring bureaucratization clearly take precedence. When this occurs, the existing bureaucracies can take the initiative quickly with little risk.

All things being equal, educational policy-makers in modern school districts are not inherently or necessarily more skilled than their counterparts in less modern districts. The process of modernization, however, gives advantages to the schoolman so that all things definitely are *not* equal. In the modern district, bias is mobilized in such a way as to give schoolmen preexisting advantages in making the important decisions about policy-making strategies and tactics.[8] Again the obstacles against a groups' successfully raising politico-moral issues are clear.

We have established a plausible though skeletal linkage between more enduring social and political factors and the results of the educational policy process. Certainly the linkage demands more attention from those who are interested in the politics of education. At the very least, indicators of such enduring characteristics must be developed. Our own work, however, has suggested that the problem may be more in gathering data and developing indicators than in finding the predicted relationships. We have shown that some of the social and political indicators that are important in community politics are also important in school district politics.

In the next chapter we try to put a little meat on this skeleton by looking at two case studies. While such case studies have limited use, they can be suggestive. First, we can get a better understanding of the process that links the educational policy-making process with SEP policy making. Second, we can develop richer insights into the tension between bureaucracy and participation, discussed in this and earlier chapters.

7

Sex Education in Anaheim and Statetown: Two Case Studies

Case studies provide a valuable addition to our survey data by allowing us to test hypotheses generated from the survey using a second, albeit less systematic, kind of data. We collected data about a sex education controversy in a single community and assembled data for a second case study using secondary sources. We are able to report on two different types of controversies; in one community, schoolmen chose a containment strategy of conflict management, and in the end the SEP was actually expanded. In the other community, schoolmen became overt partisans, the issue was never removed from the public arena, and finally the sex education program was virtually wiped out.

Our case studies focus on Anaheim, California, and a small Midwestern community that we call Statetown. Anaheim is a large community on the outskirts of Los Angeles that has experienced tremendous population growth in the last twenty years. The Anaheim sex education controversy was widely discussed in the education media and is the primary focus of Mary Breasted's book *Oh! Sex Education.*[1] Most of the data for our report on Anaheim are drawn from her account of the controversy. The study of Statetown was performed by one of the authors.[2]

Anaheim

A formal program of family life sex education began early in Anaheim. According to all accounts, the Anaheim Union High School District began this program in 1962 in an attempt to systemize certain instruction being carried out by the school nurses and the physical education staff. The early development of the Anaheim SEP is interesting because it parallels our observations in other communities: sex education started, citizens complained, an advisory committee was formed, and sex education instruction was expanded and organized as a formal program. Later controversy led to a second consideration of the program. Our focus is on the second consideration, which began in 1968.

The first controversy over sex education occurred in 1962, when some Anaheim parents complained about a film, shown by a coach, which discussed masturbation, one of the more sensitive topics in sex education. After hearing the complaints, the district board suspended such teaching and appointed a committee of schoolmen and civic leaders involved with youth problems to consider the whole question of sex education. That committee studied the issues and ran a survey in the community. The survey showed overwhelming support for sex education. The program was begun soon thereafter and by 1968 had become a national model of sorts. It was mentioned in several national publications; Mrs. Sally Williams, the program director, had become a director of the national organization SIECUS. Paul Cook, the district superintendent, had also become national figures in the pro-sex-education circles.

The second Anaheim controversy over sex education developed during the 1968-69 school year. When the year was over, several incumbents on the board of trustees had lost their positions, leading to a change in the board's character. Paul Cook, who had watched the district grow from its postwar infancy, had resigned as superintendent, and the sex education program was virtually abolished.

Breasted's View of the Anaheim Controversy

It is not clear whether there was any single precipitating factor in this second controversy. Mary Breasted quotes Sally Williams as saying that the community became aware of the way in which masturbation was treated in the program and that this was what set off the opposition. For her own part, Breasted provides at least three explanations. Much of her book employs a status politics model and focuses on the national publicity the SEP had received as a precipitating event. Her explanation requires accepting the assumption that Cook and Williams were the primary objects of the opponents' concern. "At bottom it was populism that they preached. And they made Paul Cook and Sally Williams into symbols of the detested professional elite, and went after them with the fury of the dis-possessed."[3] Having discussed the status politics model above, those arguments need not be repeated here. We contend that by relying on this perspective the opponents of a policy are by innuendo accused of acting nonrationally. Their concerns are portrayed as based on deep-seated anxieties or neuroses rather than on actual policy concerns. Breasted's status model does accurately describe the supporters of sex education as authorities and the opponents as challengers to that authority. But the status model does not accurately describe the sort of moral conflict that she found and that we outlined above in Chapter 3.

Breasted also suggests the presence of a right-wing press as a causal factor in the Anaheim controversy. The *Anaheim Bulletin* took a strong editorial position against the SEP, and a *Bulletin* writer became a West Coast anti-sex-education spokesman. Some of the local proponents felt that the *Bulletin* was the primary source of opposition to sex education and that the *Bulletin's* position was derived from a general opposition to public education by its editor, Sam Campbell.[4]

Finally, Breasted found core leadership for the opposition to sex education drawn from the California Citizens' Committee. This committee had been established in the early sixties to promote Barry Goldwater's presidential candidacy, and it had continued to exist after the election. While Breasted recognized the importance of this group in drawing attention to sex education and promoting opposition to the program, she noticeably underplays the significance of interest group politics in Anaheim and opts instead for the status politics model and a view of the California Concerned Citizens as using sex education for group maintenance purposes. Yet, it is clear from other comments in her study that there were significant general policy differences separating supporters and opponents of sex education in Anaheim and that these policy differences transcended differences over both status and sex education.

Thus, Breasted provides three hypotheses concerning the causes of the Anaheim controversy: the opponents were upset about the content or presumed content of the program; the opponents felt status deprivation and lashed out at the symbols of a status system that had passed them by; the opponents were used wrongly by certain leaders. None of these hypotheses necessarily contradicts another. However, their statement and interrelationships need clarification for them to be useful as parts of a more general theory of community conflict.

Moral Conflict in Anaheim

The conflict in Anaheim had three elements likely to be found in any community conflict: policy, object, and leadership. The *policy* issues in the Anaheim controversy revolved around the fundamentalist, conservative ideology of the opponents. They viewed sex education and other school policies as opposed to what their conservative ideology suggested as major school direction. They may not have understood the goals of sex education (as Breasted sometimes suggests), or they may have understood them all too well. They seemed to sense that sex education was related to an approach centered on a rationalist morality of consequences. The opponents clearly saw this as opposed to their own moral fundamentalism, which prescribed conduct in an absolute fashion. Yet Breasted demonstrates a blind spot toward this concern. Rather than looking at the opponents' morality as a possible legitimate starting point for controversy, she regularly seeks to explain their behavior either in terms of pathologies or ulterior motives. Thus, Breasted spends countless pages suggesting that opponents had not always practiced the morality they were supporting. She treats the California Concerned Citizens as blind followers of a fanatical leadership.

Even though she misses the moral and ideological nature of the Anaheim conflict, Breasted still points to it in her discussion of status politics. She notes that the opponents viewed people like Paul Cook and Sally Williams as part of a liberal establishment. By extension one can infer that the liberal policy promoted by Cook and Williams could as easily be the basic target of the conservative opposition. If the opponents saw the conflict in ideological terms, so did proponents of sex education. Paul Cook and Sally Williams both came to see themselves as leaders of a liberal crusade. When the program came under attack, they failed entirely to grasp the fact that sex education, by its very nature, raised moral issues. Their response was to brand the opposition as conservative "fanatics" and to suggest that opposition to sex education was part of a John Birch Society plot. The proponents, however, did not view their own position as value-based even though they seemed to grasp, but not accept as legitimate, the value basis of the opposition.

Any community controversy requires an *object*, something tangible. The need arises because the public seems almost incapable of dealing with abstractions. In William K. Muir's case study of conflict in New Haven, it was the physical presence of the metal houses which set off opposition to a zoning variance.[5]

There were two objects involved in the Anaheim controversy, the most obvious being the sex education program itself. This was one of several public school programs that represented to the conservative opponents education focused on "life adjustment." They might have based their opposition on any number of such programs in the schools. But in Anaheim, sex education was carried out as part of a highly structured, well-coordinated, and bureaucratized program. Moreover, the Anaheim SEP had received widespread attention in the national press.

The second object of the Anaheim controversy was the decision-making authority in the schools. Superintendent Paul Cook and some school board members strongly and publicly supported sex education. In many ways, Cook in particular came to embody sex education and the education for "life adjustment" that the SEP implied; he had earned a national reputation as an educator partly because of the Anaheim SEP. But while it was natural for him publicly to support the program, Cook thereby confused his authority role with his partisan role and transformed himself into a personification of the evil the program implied to the opponents. In addition, Cook openly antagonized the opposition, creating further antagonism toward the program, thereby widening the split on the issue and probably making impossible any incremental adjustment in the conflict.

Conflict requires *leadership* if it is to be sustained. In Anaheim there was leadership on both sides. While Cook sought to lead the proponents, he didn't seem to have a following. It was as if the parents who had said that they favored sex education in the 1962 opinion survey had all moved away; none emerged publicly to support the embattled school superintendent. Rather, his support was among school board members and teachers.

The opposition, on the other hand, had much public support, most effectively in the *Anaheim Bulletin*. The newspaper served as a continuing source of information and opinion for the opponents. It kept communication about sex education flowing through the community and kept the story in the news. Had the *Bulletin* buried the story the opposition probably would not have grown strong enough to make its position into public policy.

There was another important source of opposition leadership and organization in Anaheim: the California Citizens' Committee. One of its leaders, James Townsend, emerged as the first public opponent of the Anaheim program. The California Citizens' Committee disseminated opinions to its members and served as an organized core of opposition to the program.[6]

Earlier we discussed the various strategies available to schoolmen facing opposition to sex education. In the 1962 Anaheim controversy, the schoolmen had been able to deal with the opposition by appointing a blue-ribbon committee. The result was similar to most first-round considerations—the program was formalized and expanded. Paul Cook and the board of education were unable to contain the conflict during the second round in 1968.

*The Mismanagement of
Conflict in Anaheim*

The first public indication of an impending controversy over sex education came when James Townsend demanded at a regular board meeting that the authorities look into the SEP. Similar demands by other parents were made at succeeding meetings, until the board had no apparent choice and held a special meeting on the SEP. This provided the opponents with a public platform to transmit their views to the community, thereby acting to highlight and legitimize the controversy. The opponents made an effective presentation. Part of the presentation included "a slide show and a tape-recorded narration to go with it."[7] For Paul Cook and his board supporters, the meeting turned out to be a "no-win" proposition. The opponents had been allowed to state their case and give their reasons publicly.

To make matters worse, the schoolmen adopted a foolish strategy at the meeting. They could have heard out the opponents, taken the issue under advisement, studied the question with the help of interested members of the community, issued a public report, and then gone on with their business. This is the familiar public relations strategy we have found in other communities. However, the superintendent and his board supporters did not do this; rather, they debated the opponents and sought to protect their program. This may be one key to understanding what ensued. The Anaheim schoolmen had become so tied to the SEP that they were unable to allow it to be reviewed. Criticism of the program became, in their minds, criticism of them. Hence, their success in building an SEP and the national recognition they had received seemed to force them into partisan roles and made them give up the public relations strategy that had served their interests in 1962.

These were the basic elements of the Anaheim controversy. The opposition was led by an organized group, the California Citizens' Committee. The opposition was given a forum in the local press and at school board meetings. The opposition was able to personify its position by attacking the incumbent superintendent, who emerged early as the major defender of the program. The superintendent, in turn, was unable to muster vocal public support for the program, even though he had a 1962 survey that showed almost overwhelming support for sex education—in the abstract, however, and not necessarily for the program, especially as depicted by the opponents. And, since he had chosen to enter into conflict rather than to manage it, his fate was tied up with that of the SEP. At the next school board election those candidates who supported sex education lost and what had been an extensive SEP was virtually eliminated from the Anaheim schools. Paul Cook lost, too, and was forced into early retirement.

Statetown

Statetown is a small Midwestern city dominated by a large state university. It would seem improbable that a conflict over sex education or over any progressive educational issue would occur in such a community. However, a conflict did occur, and it took on a dimension not found in many other school controversies.

According to our informants the idea of developing an integrated family life program was first proposed by the Statetown PTA; the school administration then took the idea to the board. During the 1966-67 school year, the school board approved a pilot family life and sex education program for 1967-68. This occurred after the idea had been considered by a citizens' group consisting of local religious and educational leaders, including a professor of family life education from the state university.

The pilot program, limited to the seventh grade, was required of all students unless their parents specifically requested that their children not take the program (an "opt-out" program). Two teachers were assigned to the program, given released time during 1966-67, and were sent for special training to prepare them.

Other things happening in the Statetown schools at about this time would later feed the controversy over sex education. The superintendent of the district for nearly two decades resigned. The board of education had become dissatisfied with his leadership and felt that he was not innovative enough and that he lacked the will or ability to promote progressive educational ideas. Too, the community and the school board had changed markedly in the sixties because of two independent forces. Because of numerous consolidations, the school district had expanded well beyond the city limits. Statetown itself had also experienced a precipitous increase in population, due primarily to growth of the university, which more than doubled its enrollment during the decade.

These two changes had disrupted the prevalent politics of the school district. Those politics had been under the control of the superintendent, who selected candidates for the board with the covert assistance of local party leaders. By 1969 this procedure was no longer workable, for the superintendent was confronted by board opposition led by a person who had been head of the local teacher's association. This reflected another change in the composition of the board itself, which had previously tended to represent the local establishment, but now represented emerging forces in the community. When the establishment lost control of the board, the university people took control, and by the time the superintendent resigned, every board member in some way could be connected to the university.

This change is important, because it represented a basic change in philosophy on the board. The school board now demanded progressive, liberal educational policy and clearly expected the superintendent to exert leadership in making such policy. At the same time, the changes in the district suggest a basis upon which conflict over policy-making authority could develop.

The new policy orientation of the board was reflected in their choice of a new superintendent with well-established liberal credentials. He came from the superintendency of a West Coast urban district where he had gained attention by developing innovative programs that ultimately became statewide standards. When he came to Statetown, the new superintendent said that he wanted to "get out of politics and back into education." That, of course, proved to be impossible. He brought many of his earlier objectives with him, and these crystallized some underlying discontent in the district, particularly his policy of actively seeking minority candidates for teaching positions in a community with a surplus of qualified teachers anxiously seeking employment.

Things did start moving once the new superintendent arrived. The pilot sex education program was deemed successful by the board and administration, and a regular program was begun in 1968-69 with the same two teachers. In addition, other innovations were emerging, most notably the abolition of letter grades on a pilot basis in one school. The university people on the board of education were favorably predisposed toward the abolition of grades, since the university's schools had conducted a successful experiment with this policy. It is not clear whether the new superintendent actually took the lead in these changes, but that is not as important as the fact that people in the community perceived him to be the leading proponent of liberal innovations in the schools.

The Morality of Consequences

The first action leading to public controversy over sex education occurred near the end of the 1969-70 school year. One of the sex education teachers, whom we shall refer to as Mr. Young, asked the students to submit questions about sex and family life. Sex education teachers commonly employ this as a strategy to elicit topics for discussion and to overcome students' shyness about asking fairly explicit things. Many of the questions submitted by the Statetown seventh-graders were written in gutter language and dealt with topics that might shock many people. Over the summer Mr. Young collated, typed, and dittoed the questions. At the beginning of the 1970-71 school year, this list of questions was returned to the students who had submitted them with the suggestion that they take the questions home and discuss them with their parents. This simple act precipitated the conflict that would ultimately reach the courts and the state education department.

As one informant put it, when those questions went out, "All hell broke loose." For several days, a standard greeting in Statetown was "Have you seen the sex questions?" Discussion of the questions was especially intense within the Tuesday Morning Club, a group of women with mostly conservative leanings who gathered weekly at each other's homes to talk about the schools. If there was leadership in the anti-sex-education forces, it emerged from this group.

The Tuesday Morning Club had been concerned about the direction the schools seemed to be taking in Statetown. The members of the club were already upset by the prospect of letter grades being abolished, when the distribution of the student's sex questions took place. The group then came to focus their attention primarily on the sex education curriculum. The Tuesday Morning Club had some tenuous contacts with the radical right. One person regularly distributed John Birch Society literature at the club's meetings. This literature apparently did raise some questions about the SEP in other member's minds. However, the majority of those who attended the Tuesday morning meetings found the literature distasteful, and the person was asked to stop bringing it. Some other members had identifiable conservative contacts, but apparently they became acquainted with people outside of the community concerned about sex education only after the issue had been raised by "the sex questions."

Opposition Strategies and Objectives

Three public actions followed the distribution of this list:
1. A school board meeting to discuss the issue was held with 350 to 450 citizens in attendance.
2. A petition was circulated asking that the program be discontinued.
3. A suit was filed naming the teacher who had distributed the questions, the school superintendent, the board of education, and the state superintendent of schools as defendants. Plaintiffs sought injunctive relief and asked the court, essentially, to terminate the program.

The more active opponents came away from the special meeting feeling that the superintendent was going to have sex education in the schools no matter what the community felt. They also felt that they had been treated in a cavalier fashion by the superintendent at this meeting. Hence, opposition to sex education became mixed with opposition to the existing form of educational policy making.

The public meeting helped to make Mr. Young a salient issue. Prior to this time there had been some rumors concerning his radical life style. Those attending the meeting probably felt that the rumors were confirmed by his appearance. A member of the school board described his appearance: "Mr. Young has full hair, beard and so on. He had on a sweatshirt and dungarees; if his hair had been combed that week, it must have been early in the week." Another informant mentioned a band jacket as part of Mr. Young's apparel.

Nothing was done, by the school board at least, as a result of the public meeting. Mr. Young continued to teach in the SEP, and no changes in the program were contemplated by the board. In fact, plans went forward to expand the program into the senior-high-school curriculum. However, many citizens, especially the Tuesday Morning Club, were still concerned about sex education.

The source of the petition, signed by ninety-six citizens, demanding an end to the SEP is unclear. It had little immediate effect except to let the board know that some people were concerned both about the program and its teaching methods. Within the community it served the purpose of identifying individuals who were willing to take a public stand on the issue.

As with the petition, it is not clear exactly how the civil suit was started or who did it. The suit involved ninety plaintiffs and one attorney, C.D. Turner, who donated his services; some have hypothesized that he may have initiated the action himself. The list of plaintiffs appeared to have been taken directly from the signators of the petition. Several people apparently were listed as plaintiffs without their knowledge, since when the list of plaintiffs was made public, some people asked to have their names removed from the suit. One person was in the disturbing position of suing herself, since she was a member of the school board. As a legal resource, the civil suit was useless. All of the attorneys involved, including Mr. Turner's law partners, felt that the suit did not have a chance. In fact, the plaintiffs lost every time they went to court. The courts consistently ruled that the plaintiffs had recourse through the ballot box and that the issue was not judiciable.

As a political device, however, the use of the courts was a brilliant strategy, for several reasons. The civil action could be used as a bargaining point with the school board. The suit also cemented together those involved as an interest group. It provided an on-going focus of group involvement, which is often lost in such community controversies. The plaintiffs no longer had just a common interest; they were now involved in a common action. All of this provided an involved opposition beyond the membership of the Tuesday Morning Club. The suit also provided favorable publicity for the opponents of sex education. By bringing suit, the opponents were assured of press coverage. The opponents were thus able to question board policies without resorting to mass actions that might have cast them in an unfavorable light in the press. (Reporting in the local newspaper was generally slightly biased in favor of sex education.) In sum, the use of litigation presented to the community the image of a sizable number of citizens who were concerned about school policy and seeking to voice their concern through legitimate channels.

As the controversy progressed, opposition appeared to become primarily oriented toward personal issues. In particular, Young had caused many parents to become concerned about life style issues. The president of the school board was approached by Turner with an offer to drop the suit if Young were dismissed. This offer was not accepted or formally discussed by the board, since the general feeling was that Young had done nothing wrong. It was clear at this point that the board and the administration were willing to support Young and his teaching methods while ignoring his radical life style. But from this point on, the center of controversy was to be Young, rather than sex education.

Ten days before the civil suit was to go to court Young invited some members of the local Gay Liberation Front to speak to his sex education class. For him this was simply the continuation of a strategy of having all points of view on sexual-moral issues presented; he would later argue that Gay Liberation was balanced with an earlier presentation by fundamentalist clergymen. But in this action Young violated two written school policies. He did not notify the building principal that the speakers would be in the school, and he permitted (knowingly or not) certain printed material to be distributed to the class. It was the latter, apparently innocent, action which sparked new controversy. The material in question was simply a card indicating that if more information was desired, it could be gotten from "Jerry," with Jerry's telephone number listed. Young later argued that he had no knowledge of how the cards got into students' hands. Gay Liberation members told the board of education that they had simply left them on a desk and students spontaneously distributed them. At any rate, the board had a firm policy against any outside literature (including military recruiting material) being distributed in the schools. The school board now had a legal basis upon which it could act if it chose without referring directly to Young's unsettling appearance and life style.

The second round had clearly begun. The board of education immediately started receiving phone calls about the Gay Liberation presentation. During the first round, the central administration and the board had supported Young's teaching methods. One could presume that they would have continued this support if his judgment and timing had been different. The subsequent actions of the board and the administration indicated that they felt Young was now the central element in the controversy. Gay Liberation had visited the classroom on a Thursday, and by the next Monday morning Young was relieved of his teaching responsibilities and assigned to work at the board offices. The school administration and the board clearly had come to the conclusion that it was no longer possible to support Young.

The opposition filed a supplemental pleading to their suit accusing Young, the building principal, the superintendent, and the board of education of "corrupting the morals of minors." The court was asked for injunctive relief and a determination whether criminal charges should be brought against any or all of the defendants. The prosecuting attorney was not in sympathy with the plaintiffs; thus, they seemed to want the court to force him to act, a virtually unheard of order.

At first the school board vacillated. It informed Young that his contract would probably not be renewed, and in a closed session it did vote against renewal. Then Young requested a public hearing, and the board met in public to consider the renewal of his contract, with citizens speaking to both sides and some students speaking in Young's defense. Following that meeting, the board reversed itself and voted for renewal, with the stipulations that Young would not teach in the SEP and that no student would be required to take a course from him. The superintendent supported Young throughout this phase of the controversy.

At this point, the board appointed another citizens' advisory committee to consider the SEP. The committee majority strongly endorsed both the need for the program and its specific implementation and also suggested that the "subject matter" be extended to grades K-12. A short minority report dealt with the content and name of the program, suggesting that the title "Family Living" was inappropriate, since the program seemed to be primarily an SEP. The minority also questioned the opt-out nature of the eighth-grade segment of the program and suggested that the course ought to be elective with parental approval.

Results of the Controversy

The chronology of the sex education controversy in Statetown actually stops at this point, although the SEP was continued and expanded. However, it is worth following Young's case and its conclusion because some of the events add to the overall picture of the conflict. The next year (1971-72) Young was assigned to teach a special class designed to keep potential dropouts in school, an obvious choice because of his good rapport with students. However, his unconventional methods brought him trouble again. With the permission of the building principal he allowed the students to furnish and decorate their classroom. Rather than desks, straight chairs, and tables, the room was furnished with mattresses and other more comfortable furniture. The room was due for repainting and the principal gave Young permission to allow his students to paint or write on the walls. Some of the things which appeared on the walls of the classroom were obscene.

Several of the more conservative school watchers (either members or peripherally connected to the Tuesday Morning Club) heard about the classroom through the student grapevine. They entered it one day, took pictures of the furnishings and the words written on the walls, and then proceeded, using this evidence, to demand that Young be removed.

In the meantime, other things had happened in the community. In a school board election held that fall, there were clearly drawn liberal-conservative lines. Sex education was not the major issue in the election, although most of the candidates had a position in the issue. The major issue involved style of education. The more conservative candidates argued for the primacy of the "Three Rs." They opposed education for life adjustment, of which sex education was a part, as was abolition of letter grades. These candidates were generally anti-administration, while their opponents were primarily supportive of administration policies.

The school board election was no more exciting than most such elections. The candidate with the most votes in the seven-way race for three seats was an administration opponent who had signed the minority report of the citizens' advisory committee on sex education. This candidate spoke out against what she perceived to be an emphasis "on life adjustment, rather than subject matter, in the classroom" and a too rapid pace of innovation. The other winning candidates reflected the same moderately conservative views.

This election marked a change of direction in the Statetown schools. Just two weeks after the election, Young was suspended from his position and, after several appeals and public hearings, was fired permanently. Two days after Young's suspension (which was a two-day suspension at first), the superintendent resigned to return to California. He stated that the election had no effect upon his decision, and other knowledgeable people confirmed this. It is important to note, however, that the new board was not expected to support his generally liberal, social activist philosophy, and therefore Statetown was no longer as inviting an alternative for him.

The Controversy in Retrospect

The Statetown controversy involved several elements. Each must be explored individually in order to determine the sources of the controversy. Many parents were honestly concerned about the teaching of sex education in the public schools. Several opponents objected to no more than the opt-out provision in the program. Their concerns were supported by the more radical conservatives, who supplied literature opposing the SEP from outside the community. These local opponents were disturbed about sex education before they became aware of, and developed contacts with, national groups opposing sex education.

When the sex education issue arose, it became oriented toward a particular teacher who quickly personified the issue. None of the other teachers in the program was ever mentioned by the opponents. This diverted attention from the program to the teacher, so that opponents could be satisfied finally by the removal of the offending teacher. It is possible that Young personified the sort of morality we hypothesized that the opponents object to in sex education; his teaching in the SEP was based upon a morality of consequences. Young's appearance and rumored life style added to the opponents' fears about what he taught. Finally, the school board was found to deal with the morality question when the opponents documented obscenities printed on the classroom walls.

Several of the opponents were motivated by the much broader question of the purposes of the schools. Were the schools to teach basic subject matters, or were they to provide social service to the community by preparing students for life adjustment? Both sex education and Young's inquiry approach to teaching were associated with education as life adjustment. The concurrent experiments with no-grading and minority hiring also fit into this perspective.

Finally, the teaching of sex education and Young were probably nothing more than symbolic issues in the community (objects of controversy). The controversy was primarily a reaction against the new superintendent of schools. The old superintendent had viewed his role as that of a politico—getting to know the local opinion leaders, providing multiple channels of input into school decision making, never pushing very hard lest some interest be offended. In sum, he provided consensual leadership. But both the old superintendent and the school board agreed in time that he had to go because the pace of change in the schools had been too slow. When the new superintendent arrived, change seemed to take place at a rapid pace.

The push for faster change was reflected in the composition of the school board at the time of the old superintendent's resignation. The old pattern of school board selection had broken down. In the past, the superintendent had been able to select a board with the concurrence of local elites. His inability to continue this practice was a symptom of the disintegration of the consensus that had governed school politics in Statetown.[8]

The new superintendent was unwilling to rebuild the consensus. Many of his statements reflected a sense that the schools had a social responsibility to the community, *yet many influentials and a majority of the electorate did not support this philosophy.* In addition, the new superintendent tended to appear as an autocrat in the eyes of both influential members of the school administration and to people in the community.

The data from our survey of school districts showed that sex education controversies are generally episodic and that the opposition is rarely effective in either stopping or limiting programs. In this sense, the Statetown case is no exception. After the new superintendent resigned and Young was fired, the civil suit was dropped and the conflict over sex education was over without any change in the stated policy of the school district. The SEP opponents would appear to have lost, since sex education was still being taught and there was consideration of expanding it into the high-school curriculum. The only change was that students were not required to take the courses with an opt-out provision; but even with the new elective arrangement, enrollment remained virtually the same.

When Young was removed from the scene, the primary object of concern had disappeared. Many parents continued to have misgivings about the program, but those feelings were difficult to articulate and had no specific focus.

It is doubtful that there would have been a sex education conflict in Statetown if there had not been a peculiar convergence of elements: a teacher whose teaching strategy and life style were unconventional, a superintendent who believed that the schools had a duty to be involved in social change, and a community in transition that was uncertain about what it expected from its schools. The last two elements, together, caused the conflict; the first caused it to focus on sex education. Young and his approach to teaching sex education provided the object around which deeper and more abstract causes of conflict could focus.

Comparison of the Anaheim and Statetown Cases

Reports of case studies provide real-life dramas to what might otherwise be an academic and sometimes sterile exercise, albeit an important one, in hypothesis testing. However, there is fairly general agreement that a single case study contributes little to the advancement of knowledge. Thus, we chose to do comparative case studies.

We felt at the very beginning of our research that the Anaheim controversy would need to be dealt with in any lengthy report on sex education controversies. Mary Breasted's book appeared soon after we began our own research, and we found it to be a valuable source of information. However, as we began to analyze our own data we became more and more aware that many of the inferences from Breasted's book were incorrect. We finally concluded that the Anaheim controversy was atypical. Yet, it had been discussed at length. For this reason we felt compelled to treat it at greater length than we had initially planned.

While working through the two case studies we found important similarities and differences between the controversies in Statetown and Anaheim. It is these differences which make the Statetown controversy typical and the Anaheim controversy atypical.

Major Differences Between Anaheim and Statetown

Most sex education controversies result in continuation or expansion of programs (Figure 5-1). The Statetown controversy resulted in expansion, while the Anaheim controversy resulted in the elimination of the program. In Statetown, public interest focused on the methods and tactics of a particular teacher and seemed to be combined in part with opposition to the incumbent superintendent. It was difficult to differentiate generalized public opposition to the superintendent and the overall thrust of his policies from a separate concern about sex education. The controversy was ended when the two individuals who were offensive to the opposition left the scene. In Statetown attention never focused on the major question of whether sex education should be taught, and there was never a clear public input on that question. The result was minor policy adjustment of the sort that we saw in most communities.

In Anaheim such incremental changes were not possible. The opposition was motivated primarily by a basic concern about sex education in the schools. The Anaheim opponents could not be mollified by minor tinkering with the program, for they wanted the program abolished. District staffing was affected by the controversy; but in Anaheim staffing questions seemed to result from the furor over sex education rather than helping to generate it.

In Statetown, incremental and public relations strategies were emphasized throughout the controversy. The school board dealt with the question of a particular teacher rather than the program itself. When the controversy became intense, the board was able to move him out of the program. At the same time, the informal communications between the board and the leaders of the opposition seemed to indicate that this had become the opposition's major concern and that they continued to focus on the policy solely as a vehicle for pressuring the board on a personnel decision. The board also adopted the strategy of willingness to review the policy and appointed an advisory committee for that purpose almost as soon as the issue arose.

In Anaheim, on the other hand, the schoolmen adopted an entirely different strategy. Paul Cook and some board members seemed unable to believe that people would oppose the SEP. Thus, rather than seeking to apply public relations tactics to the issue in Anaheim, schoolmen took on partisan roles from the outset, and they never sought to take the question out of the public arena. This difference in approach is important, because schoolmen in both communities were convinced on the basis of opinion surveys that majorities supported sex education. Yet, in both cases the survey data were misleading, because respondents had been asked to respond to an abstract question. The implications of the programs, particularly in terms of the moral issues raised by the opponents, were not pointed out within the survey instruments (Chapter 1). It is clear in retrospect that sizable numbers of people in both communities were unwilling to support the programs when the moral issues were raised.

These distinctions point to the basic difference between the two controversies, which in turn may explain why the conflict in Anaheim was rancorous. The conflict in Statetown involved questions of authority, whereas the Anaheim conflict involved questions of ideology which came to involve basic questions of authority. In Statetown, the sex education controversy was symptomatic of a disintegration of existing authority patterns in the community. The resolution of the sex education controversy was coterminous with what people in the community perceived to be a change in authority patterns in school policy making.

The opponents in Anaheim were motivated by intertwined authority and ideological concerns. Anaheim had a history of ideological politics. Indeed, the California Citizens' Committee existed to work for conservative causes beginning with the Goldwater campaign. The ideologically conservative opposition in Anaheim was focused in two directions. Most important, it was focused on the issue of sex education. The Anaheim conservatives mirrored the model of fundamentalist opposition to sex education that we discussed in Chapter 1. Sex education in the public schools was anathema to the basic moral beliefs of the Anaheim opponents. Thus, they could not accept continuation of the program in any but emasculated form. The ideological nature of the conflict also involved competition for authority. The conservative opponents in Anahein focused their opposition on the policy-making authority of the liberal school board and superintendent and sought to replace those authorities with ideologically conservative policy makers.

The question of authority was clearly different in the two communities studied. In Statetown the question evolved primarily from a change in the way things were decided. In Anaheim the question of authority emerged from a clear ideological split; liberals controlled the school district and the conservatives didn't like it. When the conservatives gained control toward the end of the controversy, the liberals founded their own interest group to fight back.

*Similarities between Anaheim
and Statetown*

The sex education controversies in Anaheim and Statetown involved similar moral issues even though there were other, possibly more important considerations in Statetown. Our model of the moral issues involved with sex education was developed partly from an analysis of the Anaheim controversy. In Anaheim the opponents viewed the SEP as amoral (at best) since it did not explicitly teach the Judaeo-Christian moral prescriptions surrounding sex. The Anaheim proponents sought the same results in terms of students' sexual behavior but believed that a rationalist rather than a prescriptive approach was more likely to achieve that end.

In Statetown the controversy never focused upon the SEP as a transmitter of a morality of consequences. Opposition focused upon Young's explicit use and belief in the rationalist approach to sexual issues. Because Young was so easily identified with "the new morality" he became the target of opposition, thus diverting attention from the SEP as a whole.

In both Statetown and Anaheim the impetus for the program came from within the school bureaucracy. And the public "support" was neither vocal nor active; rather, it existed in a passive and abstract sense. There were no lay supporters in either community who would come forward to do continuing battle with the critics.

Public meetings occurred in both communities as a result of public opposition. Our survey data did not allow us to pinpoint the directionality of this correlation, and we considered the hypothesis that the use of public meetings might be a simple strategic blunder in schoolmen's thinking. The case studies confirm our conclusion that public meetings and other such participatory devices are used in response to strong public opposition and that public consideration without the concurrent use of a conflict containment strategy, such as appointment of a study committee, may lead to defeat of a controversial proposal.

In Statetown and Anaheim, opposition leadership was available. In Anaheim the leadership was provided by James Townsend and Sam Campbell, conservative political activists. Townsend and Campbell had the time to devote to the controversy, and each could see some benefit in it beyond simply defeating sex education. Townsend needed to keep active his organization, the California Citizens' Committee, and sex education was a useful issue. Campbell, whom Breasted describes as a "participatory journalist," needed to sell newspapers. The controversy over sex education provided local news, which, of course, is what newspapers exist on. Both Campbell and Townsend provided a continuing interest in the issue, which appears to be a major function of interest group leadership. There was also a second-level leadership in Anaheim which was energized by the two primary leaders. This consisted of members of the California Citizens' Committee who emerged as opposition spokesmen at board meetings and other public functions.

The leadership in Statetown was less visible but equally important. It is doubtful whether the opponents of sex education would have gotten beyond a few public pronouncements and a petition had it not been for the attorney, Turner, who originated the civil suit. Turner, like Townsend and Campbell, was genuinely opposed to sex education. However, it is clear from the list of defendants in his suit that he had broader political interests in the controversy. In Statetown the Tuesday Morning Club provided a second-level leadership similar to that in Anaheim. In both communities this level provided most of the activity, but its actions would have been haphazard and ineffective without the guidance of counterelites such as Townsend and Turner. Such leadership is an essential political resource. Our survey data suggest that the proponents of sex education, because they are schoolmen, generally benefit from their leadership positions. In these two communities, at least, opposition leadership was available, and an organized, continuing campaign against sex education developed.

By noting the similarities between the cadre groups in Anaheim and

Statetown we do not mean to imply that there were not also important differences between them. The Tuesday Morning Club members were for the most part moderates who were confused by Young's teaching methods and upset by his radical life style. The group had as its continuing purpose a concern about the quality of education in Statetown's schools. The California Citizens' Committee was a more rigidly ideological group which took stands not only on sex education and school policy but issues in other areas. Besides being ideologically based, this group was better organized and had a much larger membership than the Tuesday Morning Club.

Summary

Statetown and Anaheim proved to be interesting choices for comparative case studies because they had important similarities and differences. Statetown's sex education conflict was in many ways typical of what our survey data suggest as a pattern of conflict avoidance and conflict management. Statetown's schoolmen were able to remove the issue from the public arena. They almost failed because of the existence of an opposition leadership cadre and an opposition strategy to keep the issue public. The opponents, who were not motivated by an encompassing ideology, seemed to be satisfied by some minor modifications to the program and by the removal of a teacher who personified the moral issues involved with sex education. The sex education program was continued in Statetown in part because of the adoption of a public relations tactic by the proponents and in part because opposition interest was diverted from the program to a particular teacher. The Statetown controversy started because of a particular action, and the opposition, initially, was concerned about that action but not the concept of sex education. Finally, the Statetown controversy was at least intertwined with questions completely extraneous to the sex education issue.

In Anaheim the opposition adopted an all-or-nothing strategy from the outset. The opponents were not upset by a particular incident. They were upset by the program, which conflicted with their professed conservative ideology. Anaheim's schoolmen contributed significantly to their own defeat by neglecting bureaucratic methods of conflict resolution in favor of the public arena. On the other hand, our survey data suggest that the level of opposition may have precluded any other choice. As in Statetown, the Anaheim controversy spilled over into an attack on individuals. But, unlike Statetown, the individuals who came under attack were the most visible public defenders of the program and its liberal position.

Statetown and Anaheim showed some characteristics that contributed to the emergence of public controversy. There were opposition leaders with organizational and other resources available in both communities. In Anaheim and in

Statetown an organized cadre existed to carry out the day-to-day tasks of opposition.

The Anaheim controversy was atypical, because the conflict was extremely rancorous, involving an open ideological split within the community and ultimately dissolution of the SEP. The issue was not, and probably could not be, handled bureaucratically in Anaheim. The conflict in Statetown was typical of others found in our survey. The opposition was confused by a policy that it did not understand, and the issue was settled by bureaucratic methods of conflict management without significant changes in the program.

Sex Education and Social Control: Some Broader Issues in the Politics of Education

A perspective of analysis is useful if it does three things. First, it must be helpful in organizing data, in making findings appear coherent. Second, a perspective ought to provoke, to suggest insights about analogous phenomena. Third, it should stimulate further inquiry. In this final chapter we shall show the utility of the perspective that we used by evaluating it in terms of these three functions. After a brief restatement of the perspective, we shall first review the key findings in its terms. Then we shall show how useful the perspective is in explaining an analogous phenomena: how courts have dealt with the issue of sex education in the schools. Finally, we shall suggest some of the more provocative aspects of our approach. We shall do so by considering what our approach suggests about the transcending and pervasive issue of authority in school policy making.

The Perspective Restated

In the preceding chapters we have stressed the social control mechanisms that school policy-makers have at their disposal. Does this perspective bias our view of schoolmen? Most surely it does if *bias* is taken to mean that some characteristics and phenomena receive more emphasis than others. That is indeed the strength of our approach, especially because the mechanisms that we stress frequently receive too little attention. William Gamson defends this social control perspective in the following way:

> [We] would have to admit some justice to the charge that authorities have not fared very well in this treatment. . . . Control has a pejorative ring, even when it is benevolently motivated. . . . The emphasis on control comes from a focus in this book on decisions involving conflicts of interest and values. The other kinds of decisions, those involving collective interests and shared values, exist and are certainly worthy of discussion. If authorities are treated as "controllers" here, they are certainly given their due as "leaders" elsewhere.[1]

The perspective is more than just heuristically useful in the methodological sense of the word. It also has political implications, because it leads one to view authorities more critically. As we suggested in Chapter 2, the conventional views of the opposition in such issues as sex education tend to use social theories critical of those who question the basis of authority of educational policy making. The control perspective counters the imbalance.[2] With this general defense in mind, let us consider the perspective's ability to summarize, analogize, and provoke.

Summary

In Chapter 2 we showed that sex education was seen in quite divergent ways by its most vigorous protagonists. Proponents tended to see SEP development as an issue of public mental or emotional health, the type that requires the competence of those who work professionally in this field. These proponents tended to deemphasize the moral value implications of the policy. School sex education was simply another curricular adjustment that educational authorities could and should make in response to a problem requiring a relatively high degree of technical competence.

But as we saw in Chapter 1, SEP opponents viewed the issue in a completely different light. School sex education was not at all simply an issue of health but of morality, for the operating assumptions of SEPs threatened traditional moral values. Such programs not only ignored traditional morality but also discussed ideas that were inimical to this tradition. The potential partisans tended to adopt this perspective.

The data in our national study cannot offer much direct evidence that these two perspectives formed the basic issues for individual school districts' policy making; however, there are some indicators that these perspectives were indeed important. This is clear in the case studies, for in both Statetown and Anaheim such diverging perspectives informed much of the political debate. Less direct evidence about the relationship between opposition and degree of participation in school SEP development suggests that the differences were often apparent in policy-making situations. Of greater significance, however, were the ways that policy-makers' social control mechanisms acted to prevent the differences from getting out of hand. Generally these mechanisms were strong enough to prevent politicomoral conflict from playing havoc with the usual way policies were made. Enduring political structures and cultures, especially the modernity of a district, created a context in which it was easier to use some of these social control techniques.

Some of our findings on the surface appear to mitigate this rather clear-cut relationship between social control and policy making. Our survey data on schoolmen attitudes about parents' role in developing SEPs suggest that there was a difference between the schoolmen's on-the-job attitudes and their normative public-relations-oriented model. But upon further reflection this does not seem to counter our other findings. First, the response to a rather abstract question about sex education participation should not hold much weight against the realities of sex education policy making as it actually took place. Second, the response itself seems consistent with the modified school-policy-making model developed in Chapter 3. The schoolman adjusts his model to the level of conflict at hand without losing control of the issue.

Schoolmen saw the need for more than usual participation, but primarily as forms of social control. This is not to say that they would have readily described their actions primarily in these terms. Still, it is clear that these policy-makers saw a need to grant more participation that was not only commensurate with the opposition but that also would *lessen* the likelihood that the issue would be seen as a basic value conflict. A school district's success in this regard was related to its ability to use control mechanisms that were tested and familiar to the policy-makers.

It is not clear from our data whether the opponents readily understood the control implications of educational policy making. This important question surely merits fuller study, but the presently available evidence leads us to doubt that opponents were thoroughly aware of control mechanisms being used against them. The ease with which SEPs were adopted is a general indicator that, despite their participatory ideology, the opponents either did not see the importance of constant surveillance over everyday educational policy making or could not do much about it.[3] Even in the case study communities, opponents seriously threatened a program only *after* it had been developed and implemented. Programs encountered more resistance when committees composed entirely of professionals were used during reconsideration. This showed that the opposition could at times successfully challenge policy-making mechanisms on the grounds that elites controlled them.

Analogies: Sex Education and the Courts

Up until now we have been concerned almost solely with the way schoolmen developed SEPs at the school district level. The social control perspective is also useful in describing how other policy-makers dealt with the issue. In the following section we shall concentrate on the courts' involvement with SEPs and show once again that problem defining and social control are intertwined.

Litigation is another way that disputes over sex education could have been settled or considered. The data we collected showed that in fact litigation was used infrequently; lawsuits on the subject were filed in only 6 percent of the districts. Furthermore, none of the national groups opposing SEPs got involved in any litigation. This absence is surprising, because the lawsuit seems to offer some especially attractive advantages to the opposition. Courts are frequently quite responsive to intense minorities who claim that the majority has illegitimately imposed its views upon them. Litigation might also be used as a form of harassment or as a means of getting schoolmen to take the opposition seriously by forcing them to include the opponents in the calculus of school policy making. (This is similar to the argument that litigation in the environmental field decreases the likelihood that industries will continue to see environmental issues as externalities.) When a school district is being sued, as was the case in Statetown, there is simply no way it can completely ignore its opposition, because it is now a formal, legal adversary. One either responds or forfeits the case. Given the advantages of litigation, it is interesting that the opponents generally failed to use this strategy. We think that a lack of financial and organizational resources and doubt that the legal process could accomplish their goals contributed to this failure.

Still, some cases on the subject have been heard before courts that publish opinions. There are not enough of these cases to allow generalizations about geographical pattern, but it may be noteworthy that three of the five cases, and the ones where the basic issues are raised most clearly, are from Atlantic Coast states. Sex education programs are common in these areas, but these areas also contain many Catholics and a tradition of litigation over state involvement with religion. The strategies involved in this litigation and the kinds of issues the litigants raised show that some individuals saw the court as a forum for the protection of a minority whose moral view is threatened by the majority. These decisions offer further insight into the relationship between the way a public policy maker, in this case the courts, defines a situation and the kinds of policy responses developed.

The perspective and values of SEP opponents did not fare very well in this litigation. In only one case was there any sign that the opponent's definition of the situation was even tentatively accepted.[4]

Two questions dominate the litigation: Is school sex education an issue of public health or morality? Can SEPs be made compulsory? From the standpoint of constitutional law, a third question is even more important: Are such programs an interference with the free exercise of religion? In the present context this question is less important, because its answer depends upon the health-morality issue.

The courts were sympathetic toward the compulsory quality of school sex education and saw the issue as one of public health education that easily fit within the curriculum expertise of school authorities. One judge put this view quite succinctly while speaking of the Maryland statute that required SEPs for all students at certain stages of their education. He noted that the program should be seen "quite simply as a public health measure."[5]

Because the courts viewed the programs as secular, they did not recognize any undue coercion on the part of the state. This follows for two reasons. First, since the programs were secular, the state was not establishing any state religion in the sense precluded by the First and Fourteenth Amendments of the United States Constitution. If the courts saw the programs in a more nonsecular light, then the burden of proof would shift overwhelmingly to the state to show that these programs were not violating some parents' rights. Because the programs were free of religious taint, they were viewed as morally neutral, and because they were neutral, the presumption of constitutionality was overwhelmingly strong.

There is evidence of neutrality in the religious sphere and only a fear that instruction in the health curriculum could possibly conflict with individual beliefs. The court cannot presume that any religious activities seep into or permeate the purposes of the curriculum.[6]

The second reason for the relationship between secular authority and social control had to do more directly with the nature of parental authority. In two recent cases, the opponents of SEPs alleged that parents have a virtually exclusive right to teach their children about sex. In both cases, the courts clearly refused to accept this view.[7]

In sum, the dominant linkage between a judge's definition of the problem and the social control mechanisms they approved for schoolmen to use is characterized by the following pattern:

1. The programs deal with secular issues or at least deal in a secular way with issues that may have some religious implications to some few people.

2. The courts defer to the expertise of curricular authorities. Therefore: the burden of proving the need for coerciveness does not fall as heavily on the states; and the harm of state coerciveness on individual conscience or morality is not great enough to warrant limits of state interference.

3. Therefore, compulsory SEPs are acceptable.

In contrast, it is worth taking a brief look at the only court case where SEP opponents met with even limited success. Their success was very tentative, because the initial decision simply staved off a summary dismissal of the case; the judge ruled that the case should go to trial. In fact, approximately one year later (1972) the opponents were still in limbo; at that time a New Jersey court dismissed the case because the opponents had not exhausted all other proper remedies prior to going to court.[8] Nonetheless, it is worth looking briefly at the judge's opinion in the initial case, because it clearly illustrates both an opposing perspective on school sex education and the implications for social control.

The judge in this case clearly saw greater moral implications in SEPs, for the school board's actions came rather close to establishing a religion. Consequently, in his view, minorities may very well have the right to be exempt from such programs. As he put it, "Plaintiff's assertion of a right to conscience is more impressive than the score card [presented at the hearing] ... that 70% of [respondents in] the Junior Chamber of Commerce Poll thought sex education was a good idea."[9]

Though litigation raises some main issues quite clearly, other social control implications were not discussed either by the courts or the adversaries.

The SEP opponents lump together all SEPs in such a way as to avoid consideration of the differences in the degrees of coerciveness. Indeed, most state education statutes allow for compulsory SEPs, and most do not allow religious exemptions.[10] Still, exceptions were regularly allowed, and in fact only two of those challenged actually involved a situation where there were virtually no exemptions. One was the New Jersey case, where the plaintiffs met with at least some tentative success. In the other cases, options were apparent. Either a student could be excused when a film on human sexuality was shown (Hawaii), or students could be excused if their parents demonstrated that they offered a sex education program at home (Connecticut).

From the opponents' viewpoint there were undoubtedly good reasons for the failure to make such distinctions or to recognize these options. First, the programs put the burden on the minority to exercise options. No one wants their children to be the ones to leave the classroom, nor are most parents likely to appreciate the need to develop and be held accountable for a study plan, however rough, for the education of his or her children. Second, the opponents were interested in imposing their own moral values on the class. There is a high degree of cant apparent in the opponents' arguments that they were simply interested in protecting their own moral values. As we described in the first two chapters, such opponents object to school sex education at least partially because it does not try hard enough to impose a traditional moral stance on everyone.

The proponents' lack of candor and the courts' unwillingness to question it are apparent in their uncompromising attitude toward opposing moralities. The actions of the New Jersey State Board of Education offer a good example. In early 1967 that board recommended the development of sex education courses. Two years later, noting conflict over the issue and wanting to investigate it, the New Jersey legislature asked the state board to declare a temporary moratorium on the development of new SEPs. The board almost immediately agreed to this recommendation, though during the moratorium the district that was later involved in a lawsuit on the issue adopted a new program. About nine months after the moratorium's inception, the legislature endorsed school sex education but suggested some limitations, one of which was to make the courses voluntary. The state board took exception to this recommendation, as well as to one asking that no such courses be offered below the junior-high level.

The board justified their actions on the grounds that excusing a student would detract from the success of the program. Students who need the program the most would not receive its benefits. No attention was given to the value implications, nor did the board recognize the possibility that some parents might see this as an encroachment of state authority. Most significant was the lack of any real attempt to show that the implementation depended upon the presence of those who would otherwise have excused themselves. In the board's opinion, since the issue was secular, the board had the authority to take such action, and no mitigating action need also be taken.

The defense of the Maryland courses also concealed its value implications.

The programs were initially developed in response to what was seen as a problem of premarital pregnancy. Pregnancy, however, is not simply a health problem. One's willingness to define premarital pregnancy as a problem depends upon a set of moral values regarding marriage and family. Surely pregnancy per se is not a problem. Thus, the early rationale for the programs suggest that they were not, as one judge defined them, quite simply public health measures. Compare, for example, the mixed health and moral issues here with the far less ambiguous health issues that are part of the rationale for compulsory smallpox vaccinations.

The perspective we adopted leads to the conclusion that the issue is indeed moral and that the imposition of values and attempts at social control ought to be reduced by both sides. This can best be accomplished by making the courses voluntary.[11] Even though the issue involves morality, it is still basically secular. More important, as the U.S. Supreme Court has argued, school policy makers cannot be coerced to eliminate programs entirely solely because some people object on religious grounds. On the other hand, for the opponents of SEP the moral implications are serious enough to threaten the free exercise of their respective religions. The proponents have not demonstrated that there is, to use a legal phrase, compelling state interest in making the courses compulsory, nor does the behavior of the opponents threaten the public peace or safety.

We reject the intolerance of the traditional either-or position, but we also reject the proponents' illusion that their approach is value free. It is more a form of political rhetoric that fosters control than a sound description of the proponents' position. As our discussion in Chapter 1 indicated, some proponents were aware of SEP's moral implications. They recognized that the programs were frequently based on some sort of situation ethics. Even this recognition, however, does not go far enough. It is one thing to recognize that the imposition and enforcement of some morality is inevitable, but it is quite another to recognize that freedom and diversity are such values, and that there is no cultural consensus over the degree to which their values should be accepted. It may be paradoxical that we discuss proponent intolerance in these terms, but it is necessary.

The issue of tolerating intolerance is a difficult one to cope with in a society that aspires to be democratic. It requires that those who advocate the values of tolerance and diversity manifest these values by protecting those who are quite intolerant of opposing views. There is no easy philosophic or political solution to the problem. The willingness to tolerate such groups might depend upon a society's aspiration and the faith it has in the strength of its own institutions. Societies with a rather stable institutional base can perhaps afford the luxury of this intolerance. In a sense, such societies might offer a lesson by example to groups most distrustful of other views. The situation may be rather different if the intolerant groups are initially so strong that this learning process has no time to take roots. With much understatement, John Rawls characterizes such a situation as one that "presents a practical dilemma which philosophy alone cannot resolve."[12]

All of this raises important questions about the relationship between authority and participation, because, as the courts' actions indicate, the definition of the situation has a great deal to say about who has authority to act, and this authority in turn can blunt other attempts at influencing the policy process. By "authority" we mean legitimate power or, more exactly, the belief among those whom one is trying to influence that the potential influencer behaves in a legitimate manner. Authority has an important advantage that other forms of power do not have because its presence increases the likelihood that a loser in a power struggle will accept the consequences.[13]

The Provocative Nature of the Perspective: Authority and Participation

The willingness to participate in politics requires a sense of political efficacy.[14] Efficacy means not only that persons feel that they can have effect on the process but may also do so legitimately. Discussions of political efficacy tend to ignore the importance of legitimacy, but our discussion of educational policy making shows that the ability to question a group's legitimacy is an important control mechanism. Legitimacy has many bases, one of which is expertise. Legitimacy based on expertise minimizes the role of lay citizen participation.[15]

Expertise is at the base of what might be called the leadership view of school policy makers' perception of SEP development (following Gamson's distinction between leadership and control, quoted earlier in this chapter). In this view, the schoolman is something like a benevolent leader who achieves consensus both because he knows what is best and because no important value conflicts are apparent. This perspective is similar to the public relations model discussed in Chapter 3. It is a perspective that writers about that model claim is typically adopted by schoolmen.

But the social control perspective suggests a quite different explanation. In this view, authorities are primarily concerned with trying to impose policies whose correctness they have already determined. Authorities use citizen participation as a means of social control or conflict/discontent management that fosters consensus by mitigating or denying basic value conflicts.

This view comes closer to understanding the oppositions' perspective of authority and participation. In Chapter 3 we argued that the groups most intensely opposed to SEPs generally included the questioning of existing authority and the broadening of participation as basic tenets of their political ideologies. That is, they tend to question the legitimacy of schoolmen's authority and their perspectives and to view issues as "political" ones requiring mass participation.

Now we have come full circle to the issues we alluded to in the introduction to this book. In that earlier discussion we asserted that our view changed as we became more aware of the similarity between schoolmen's behavior regarding traditional moralists and their behavior regarding other groups. At the very least, the social control perspective emphasizes the importance of confronting this issue. It suggests not only that basic changes in effective levels of community participation in educational policy making would clearly alter the basis of schoolman authority; it also suggests that, in some important ways, the more militant critics of the process, whether they be associated with the left or the right, are alike in the way they question this authority.

At least two responses are usually made to this conclusion. First, one might dismiss the attempts at greater participation simply because they are the products of "extremists." The issue is too important to be dismissed with that *ad hominem* argument. One can also decide to ignore the general issue of participation and support increased community control over educational policy making only on issues he or she favors. This is of course a common and tempting response, but it is limiting because it too easily dismisses the importance of the general issue. More important, such a response also limits one's abilities to see crucial links between the issue at hand and other school issues.

Thus, the social control perspective provoked us in two ways. First, it led us to question our own position on political participation. Second, it provoked us into seeing school policy making in a more comparative sense by pointing out the enduring importance of the authority-participation issue in educational politics. It is the latter issue we wish briefly to discuss now.

The issues of participation and authority link school consolidation, busing, school decentralization, and sex education; in all of these cases groups who felt that their ability to use "their" schools to perpetuate "their" values was threatened by others who defined the issue in such a way as to challenge parental authority and to impose a new set of moral values. In Ocean Hill, black parents objected to the notion that the values of most white educational administrators and teachers should dominate. In South Boston, the white parents see the issue as an attempt to destroy the communitarian function of their schools. In midwestern hamlets the objection to school consolidation frequently centered around a fear that the schools could no longer be used as a bastion against the onrushing dominant culture. The sex education controversy in Anaheim revolved around opponent fear of a changing sexual morality. In both the decentralization and consolidation cases, educators' responses were frequently the same. They stressed that "nonpolitical" issues like efficiency made it necessary to accept their own view of the problem and its solutions. Even in the busing issue there is some of this, as white ethnics refuse to accept the criteria that educators who support busing use as a basis for its defense. In sex education controversies schoolmen stressed "public health" in attempting to depoliticize the issue. Yet the opponents continued to see moral implications in public school instruction about sex.

In all of these cases the threatened groups respond by turning inward, reasserting the purity of their position, and ultimately questioning the basic structure of political authority. On the other hand, policy-makers respond in a similar fashion, describing opposition as militant, racist, or anachronistic. In attempting to maintain their authority and to avoid serious consequences resulting from the politico-moral conflict, policy-makers have responded by using counterinfluence in each case. Yet, social scientists have failed to examine critically this type of response, probably because we are, in many ways, kinsmen of the policy-makers whom we study.

These comparisons are obviously incomplete if not facile at this stage. They are not meant to be definitive, nor are they meant to offer uncritical support to community participation in all forms of educational policy making. They are simply illustrative and imply that moral conflict with the accompanying issue of political authority may be at the root of a good deal more of school politics and educational policy than our conventional wisdom or the dominant public-relations orientations of school professionals suggest.

Appendixes

Appendix A: The Data

Analysis of the Questionnaire

With the exception of Chapter 7, which reports on community case studies, the data upon which this study is based were gathered using a mail questionnaire. We adopted the questionnaire approach because of the questions we felt were of primary importance: Why did some school districts adopt sex education while others did not? Why were there sex education controversies in some districts but not in others? And why did the opponents win in some districts but not in others?

The questionnaire we developed was addressed to superintendents as community informants. In much of the content of the questionnaire we borrowed heavily from Crain, Katz, and Rosenthal's study of fluoridation controversies.[1] Crain et al. sent questionnaires to several different community informants. We were able to identify only the superintendent of schools as a possible source of information about the history of sex education in the district, including both the content of any SEP and politics related to it. Like Crain et al., we sought information about a large number of communities. Unlike those authors, we had no initial information about the existence or nonexistence of an SEP in a given district. Nor were we able to discover in advance which districts had considered sex education. We were, of course, aware of a few well-publicized controversies. But we felt that a small purposive sample would not allow us to speak to the questions raised in this book.

It is obvious that the superintendent might be a biased source of information. However, set against this was the possibility that the superintendent would have the most information about the district's curriculum, would be aware of any problems related to sex education, and would be generally knowledgeable about school district politics.

The questionnaire was divided into three major sections (see Appendix B). The first section, labeled "Superintendent Questionnaire" asked for information about the superintendent, about other curricular innovations, and about the politics (if any) of sex education in the district. We sought data about the superintendents' backgrounds in order to test hypotheses concerning the role of the education profession in diffusing sex education. Questions about other parts of the curriculum or classroom organization were included in order to test hypotheses about the relationship between consideration of sex education and innovativeness in other areas. The purpose of the questions on sex education are self-explanatory. A series of attitude questions were also included in the questionnaire to test the hypothesis that superintendents' reported attitudes about consultation with parents played a role in the way in which sex education was handled and to discover the extent to which superintendents differentiated sex education from other policy matters.

The second part of the questionnaire, labeled "Section A," asked for demographic, organizational, and historical information about the district. The data sought here were divided into two areas of inquiry: What, if any, relationship is there between organizational resources and consideration of sex education? What, if any, relationship is there between general conflict in the district and conflict over sex education?

The final section of the questionnaire, labeled "Section B," asked for specific information about the sex education program. It was necessary to collect such information because sex education can be developed incrementally. Thus, we wanted to know the relative extent of the program in terms of resources committed, topics covered, etc. We also wanted to know what, if any, changes had taken place in the program. The items in this section were developed from analyses of curricula guides from several school districts and published reports of SEPs.

The questionnaire was pretested by mailing it to a number of districts not to be included in the study population. On the basis of the pretest and Crain et al.'s experience with many of the items, we felt confident about the instrument that went into the field. Our initial confidence was on the whole justified. All but three of the items in the "Superintendent Questionnaire" were useful and valid based upon predictive tests. The only items in that part of the instrument which did not generate useful information were numbers 4, 5, and 6. Those items were intended to measure the professionalism of superintendents in qualitative terms. Respondents appeared to overstate or inflate their professional activities, and there was little variance in these data. This may have been a result of lack of specificity in the items.

"Section A" of the questionnaire proved to be disappointing, and very little of the data generated from it were used. There were no clear correlations between many of the items pertaining to staffing or budget and consideration of sex education. Nor were there correlations between the data on bond issues and consideration of sex education. Finally, there were too few reports of sex education referenda to find any meaning in those data. However, our dissatisfaction with these data may be the result of disappointment at having been unable to disconfirm null hypothesis.

We were generally satisfied with the data collected using "Section B." In fact, those data proved to be so extensive that we finally dealt only with data from B1, B2, and a recoding of B6 into "yes, it is taught" or "no, it is not taught" for each item. In essence, too much data were generated, because we were not sure at the outset about how the extensiveness of an SEP should be defined. Anyone interested in defining the average sex education program or curriculum would find these data very useful.

The Population and Response Bias

Questionnaires were mailed to superintendents of all school districts in the United States with an enrollment of five thousand or more students in 1968.[2]

We chose to send questionnaires to all of the "large" districts rather than to a sample of all districts because we felt that large districts would be more likely to have a minimum resource base sufficient to support a planned sex education program. This was important, since our primary concern was with conflict over sex education rather than whether or not districts had or had not considered sex education.

The overall response rate to the questionnaire was somewhat disappointing. Seventeen hundred and eight questionnaires were mailed, and after follow-up letters 540 districts responded, for a response rate of 31.6 percent. *Nations' Schools* conducts a regular post card survey of schoolmen and generally achieves a 60 percent response. On the two occasions prior to our survey that *Nations' Schools* dealt with sex education, the response to the post card poll rate dropped to 40 percent.[3] Our response rate, with extensive follow-up, was thus not quite as good as *Nations' Schools*. Yet, the previous experience with low response to a questionnaire dealing with sex education provided advance warning that we could not expect to achieve as high a response as some other elite and mail questionnaire studies.

The poor response rate obliged us to make a systematic search for biases in the data before proceeding with the analysis. To make comparisons between school districts that did and did not respond to the questionnaire, descriptive data were gathered about the areas in which the districts were located as well as a limited amount of data about the districts themselves. No data were available about sex education, so comparisons were made on the basis of demographic data.

The Bureau of Census does not publish statistics for school districts. In addition, few school districts in the study shared boundaries with Standard Metropolitan Statistical Areas or other governmental units. But nearly all the school districts were contained within counties, so county census data were coded for each school district to which a questionnaire was sent. The use of county data to describe school districts is not a totally satisfactory procedure, since the county is an inclusive unit and may contain several school districts, but they were sufficient for the general comparison of respondents to nonrespondents.

Response to the questionnaire varied between regions (Table A-1). We were least likely to receive responses from school districts located in the South, in the Deep South in particular. Three hundred and ten questionnaires were sent to the Deep South, and only forty-two, or 16 percent, were returned. If the South were removed from the population, the response rate would rise to 38 percent.

The South provides some interesting case studies of response and nonresponse. Questionnaires were sent to fifty school districts in Alabama, and only four useable responses were received, for a response rate of 8 percent. Three of the four districts that responded had more than ten thousand students in 1968. Only nine of the other forty-six districts had more than ten thousand students. In Mississippi two districts responded, and one of them had more than ten thousand students. Only four of the remaining twenty-five districts in Mississippi

Table A-1
Geographical Distribution of Responses

Region	Percent Returned	Number Sent
Northeast	33	114
Middle Atlantic	36	312
East North Central	40	300
West North Central	61	66
Mountain	55	71
Far West	45	247
West Border	32	151
Deep South	16	310
East Border	25	137

had more than ten thousand students. This suggests that in the South responses were biased toward larger districts. The census data tend to support this conclusion.

As the data in Table A-2 indicate, responding districts in the Deep South tended to be wealthier (median family income), somewhat more urban, and somewhat more literate (median school years completed) than nonresponding districts. We would hypothesize that the criteria for selecting school districts did not work properly in the Deep South. Southern schools are organized on a county basis. Thus, there may be numerous districts with five thousand or more students which actually do not have large budgets or staff resources which would make sex education feasible. In addition, of course, the South tends to be more characterized by the fundamentalist Protestant ethic that we hypothesized to be opposed to sex education. Responses in the South were biased toward more cosmpolitan districts and away from districts unlikely to consider sex education. Indeed, at least two southern superintendents took offense at items in our questionnaire. This is a systematic bias, but if the hypothesis is correct, then data from those districts would have served only to increase our certainty concerning hypotheses related to consideration of sex education. For example, we hypothesized a relationship between the professional-cosmopolitanism of school districts as indicated by the background of the superintendent and consideration of sex education. In Florida, which is not an educationally underdeveloped state and which does not follow the size pattern of nonresponse seen in other Deep South states, our response rate was only 22 percent. But in Florida, school superintendents are blatantly political officials and thus quite unlikely to be cosmopolitan professionals.

The same general pattern existed in our responses generally. The districts that responded were more likely to be innovative than districts that did not respond.

Table A-2

Responding and Nonresponding Districts in the Deep South (Means)

	Response	No Response
Median Family Income (1960)	$4827	$3762
Median School Years Completed by Residents 25 and Over (1960)	9.4	8.8
Percent Unemployed (1960)	6.2	5.4
Percent Employed in White-Collar Occupations (1960)	34	31

Table A-3

Responding and Nonresponding Districts Outside the Deep South (Means)

	Response	No Response
Median Family Income (1960)	$6414	$6152
Median School Years Completed by Residents 25 and Over (1960)	11.2	10.9
Percent Unemployed (1960)	5.4	5.5
Percent Employed in White-Collar Occupations (1960)	44	39

Table A-3 compares respondent and nonrespondent districts, excluding districts in the Deep South. Respondent districts are slightly more likely to be located in urban areas than nonresponding districts. Median income tends to be higher in responding districts, as does median school years completed and percent white collar.

Thus, the picture presented is one of school districts that are more likely to be middle class than most districts. Such districts are more likely to be progressive than other districts. And the districts that responded were more likely to consider adding a sex education curriculum. This is shown more directly in Table A-4, which compares the percentage of questionnaires returned from each of the nine regions to the percentage of those districts with comprehensive SEPs. The correlation (Spearman) between percent returned and percent with comprehensive SEPs is .68.

Does this bias affect the *conclusions*? We think that it does not. Our purpose at the outset was to study districts that had considered sex education. The bias is toward increasing the likelihood that districts that responded would have considered sex education. Further, the sort of bias found in these data should have no independent impact upon community conflict. Both Anaheim and Statetown, for example, are white-collar, middle-class communities, and both

Table A-4

Percent of Questionnaires Returned Compared to Percent of Responding Districts with Comprehensive SEPs

Region	Questionnaires Returned	Comprehensive SEPs
Northeast	33	23
Middle Atlantic	36	61
East North Central	40	51
West North Central	61	57
Mountain	55	33
Far West	45	51
West Border	32	36
Deep South	16	9
East Border	25	21

experienced conflict over sex education. The effect of the bias upon our conclusions is probably in the direction of forcing us to understate them. The "real" differences are most likely *greater* than our data indicate, for example, we reported that cosmopolitan-professionalism led to consideration of sex education. Yet, the data overrepresent such districts, thus decreasing the variance and forcing us to be more tentative in our conclusion about this relationship.

Appendix B: The Questionnaire

Superintendent Questionnaire

Professors Hottois and Milner
Dept. of Political Science
Grinnell College
Grinnell, Iowa 50112

INSTRUCTIONS:

Please answer all questions which apply to your district. If you are asked to answer a question which does not apply to your district, please write "not applicable." If you wish, the second part of the questionnaire ("A") may be answered by anyone who has access to information about size of teaching staffs, budget, etc.

If you wish, the third portion ("B") may be filled out by the director of Family Life/Sex Education, a curriculum director, or an assistant superintendent.

You may, of course, also fill out these sections yourself.

1. We would like to start by asking you some questions about yourself. Which of the following degrees do you hold? Check the appropriate ones. If you hold degrees in educational administration please be sure to indicate this under "major."

Bachelor   Year_____ From _____ Major_____
                             (Name of school & location)
Master   Year_____ From _____ Major_____
                             (Name of school & location)
Doctorate Year_____ From _____ Major_____
                             (Name of school & location)

2. Would you briefly describe the jobs which you have held in your career prior to becoming superintendent in this district and the years when you held them.

Years	Position	Location
EXAMPLE: 1865-90	Taught American History	Grinnell, Iowa

3. How long have you been superintendent of schools in this district? Since 19___.

4. Do you belong to any associations for school administrators? _____ No
_____ Yes How many? _____

5. Do you regularly read any professional educational journals? _____ No
_____ Yes How many? _____

6. In the past twelve months, have you attended any conventions of school administrators? _____ No _____ Yes How many? _____

7. Does your school board hold public meetings specifically or partly devoted to curricular matters?

      _____ Yes, regularly
      _____ Yes, but infrequently
      _____ No, no such meetings
      _____ Don't know

8. Does your state have any laws (e.g., statutes or court decisions) which would affect planned programs in Family Life/Sex Education? Do any of the following exist in your state? (Check all the appropriate.)

      _____ Laws *requiring* planned programs in Family Life/Sex Education
      _____ Laws *encouraging* but *not* requiring a planned program
      _____ Laws *discouraging* but *not* prohibiting a planned program of Family Life/Sex Education
      _____ Laws *prohibiting* a planned program of Family Life/Sex Education
      _____ Don't know

9. Does your state have a law requiring that if Family Life/Sex Education is taught, it be taught on a voluntary basis?

      _____ Yes _____ No _____ Don't know

10. Is there pending or has there been any litigation in your district regarding Family Life/Sex Education?

      _____ Yes _____ No _____ Don't know

11. We would like to know whether your district has tried any of the following in all or some of its schools. In the space provided please indicate (1) whether your district has tried it, (2) the year it was first tried in your district, and (3) whether there was any community opposition to the program either prior to *or* subsequent to its adoption. Do this for each of the programs.

	Tried it		Year 1st tried	Was there community opposition to idea	
	Yes	No		Yes	No
Language Labs			19___		
Full Year Plan			19___		
Flexible or Modular Scheduling			19___		
Open Classrooms			19___		
Team Teaching			19___		
Courses emphasizing "social science" instead of "social studies"			19___		

12. Has a planned program of Family Life/Sex Education ever been considered by school officials in your district?

_____ Yes _____ No (Go to Q.33) _____ Don't know (Go to Q.33)

13. Were you the superintendent when it was first considered?

_____ Yes _____ No

14. As far as you know, which was the first local organization or group to suggest a planned program of Family Life/Sex Education for the schools of your district?

15a. Did the opponents of Family Life/Sex Education at any time distribute any printed literature (pamphlets, leaflets, etc.) in your district or at a meeting?

_____ Don't know _____ No (If no, go to Q.16a) _____ Yes

15b. IF YES, did any of this literature come from outside the community?

_____ Yes, all of it
_____ Yes, some of it
_____ No, none of it
_____ Don't know

16a. Did the proponents of Family Life/Sex Education at any time distribute any printed literature?

_____ Don't know _____ No (If no, go to Q.17) _____ Yes

16b. IF YES, did any of this literature come from outside the community?

_____ Yes, all of it
_____ Yes, some of it
_____ No, none of it
_____ Don't know

In some districts, Family Life/Sex Education was considered or discussed several times. We would like to know how many times Family Life/Sex Education came up in your district and what action was taken each time. The following questions are directed to this point.

17. When was a planned program of Family Life/Sex Education first considered by school officials or discussed by groups in your district? 19___

18. At that time, was a public meeting on the subject held by the board of education?

_____ Yes
_____ No, but there was talk of holding a meeting (Go to Q.20a)
_____ No (If no, go to Q.20a)

IF YES

19. Was the sentiment of the meeting in favor of Family Life/Sex Education or against it?

_____ Against it _____ In favor

20a. During the first consideration was the matter referred to a committee?

_____ No
_____ Yes. Commmittee including only school board members and/or professional educators
_____ Yes. Committee including only laymen other than school board members
_____ Yes. Committee including both school officials and laymen.

20b. As a result of the first consideration was (Check the single most appropriate phrase)

_____ Family Life/Sex Education begun
_____ Family Life/Sex Education not begun
_____ Other, please specify

20c. If school officials decided against beginning a planned program of Family Life/Sex Education, what do you think was their *principal reason*?

_____ Other schools had not adopted
_____ Not a proper school function
_____ Public opposition
_____ Uncertainty about effectiveness
_____ Too costly
_____ Other, please specify
_____ Don't know

21. During the first consideration, what position did the board of education and the superintendent take?

Board of Education	Superintendent
_____ Favored Family Life/Sex Education	_____ Favored Family Life/Sex Education
_____ Opposed Family Life/Sex Education	_____ Opposed Family Life/Sex Education
_____ Took no stand	_____ Took no stand
_____ Urged further study	_____ Urged further study
_____ Don't know	_____ Don't know

22. Were any other public officials, individuals, newspapers, TV or other forms of mass communications, or groups important in the decision?

_____ Yes _____ No (If no, go to Q.24)

23. IF YES, which officials, individuals, newspapers, TV or other forms of mass communications, or groups, and what were their positions?

Official's title, newspaper's name, or brief description of individual or group	Favored	Opposed	Took no stand	Urged further study	Other (Specify)

24. Was Family Life/Sex Education considered a second time in your district?

_____ Yes _____ No (If no, go to Q.33)

25. In which year was Family Life/Sex Education considered for the second time? 19___

26. Was a public meeting on that subject held by the school board at that time?

_____ Yes
_____ No, but there was talk of holding a meeting (go to Q.28a)
_____ No, (go to Q.28a)

27. IF YES, was the sentiment of the meeting in favor of Family Life/Sex Education or against it?

_____ In favor _____ Against

28a. During the second consideration was the matter referred to a committee?

_____ No
_____ Yes, Committee included only school board members and/or professional educators
_____ Yes, Committee included only laymen other than school board members
_____ Yes, Committee included both school officials and laymen

28b. As a result of the second consideration was (Check the single most appropriate phrase)

_____ Family Life/Sex Education begun (go to Q.30)
_____ Family Life/Sex Education not begun
_____ Family Life/Sex Education continued as it was
_____ Family Life/Sex Education continued and expanded (go to Q.30)
_____ Family Life/Sex Education continued, but contracted
_____ Family Life/Sex Education discontinued
_____ Other, please specify

29. If school officials decided against beginning continuing, or expanding a planned program of Family Life/Sex Education the second time, what do you think was their *principal reason*?

_____ Other schools had not adopted
_____ Not proper school function
_____ Public opposition
_____ Uncertainty about effectiveness
_____ Too costly
_____ Other, please specify
_____ Don't know

30. When Family Life/Sex Education was considered for the second time, what position did the board of education and the superintendent take?

Board of Education	*Superintendent*
_____ Favored Family Life/Sex Education	_____ Favored Family Life/Sex Education
_____ Opposed Family Life/Sex Education	_____ Opposed Family Life/Sex Education
_____ Took no stand	_____ Took no stand
_____ Urged further study	_____ Urged further study
_____ Don't know	_____ Don't know

31. Were any other public officials, individuals, newspapers, TV or other forms of mass communications, or groups important in the decision?

_____ Yes _____ No (If no, go to Q.33)

32. IF YES, which officials, individuals, newspapers, TV, or other forms of mass communications or groups, and what were their positions?

Official's title, newspaper's name, or brief description of individual or group	Favored	Opposed	Urged further study	Took no stand	Other (Specify)

32a. Was a planned program of Family Life/Sex Education considered again after this?

_____ No _____ Yes (How many more times? _____)

33. Is your school board elected or appointed?

_____ Elected from single-member districts
_____ Elected at-large
_____ Appointed (If appointed, by whom_____)
_____ Other, please specify

34. Did Family Life/Sex Education ever become an issue in the election or appointment of school board members?

_____ No _____ Yes, in 19___

35. Is your school district likely to consider a planned program in Family Life/Sex Education in the near future?

_____ Yes

_____ No. In the space below please indicate why it is not likely to be considered.

_____ Don't know

36a. If your district were to consider such a planned program of Family Life/Sex Education, how much, if any, community opposition would you expect?

_____ No opposition

_____ Very little opposition

_____ Some opposition

_____ A great deal of opposition

36b. If your district is presently considering or has considered a planned program in Family Life/Sex Education how much opposition is or was there?

_____ No opposition

_____ Very little opposition

_____ Some opposition

_____ A great deal of opposition

37. Do you agree or disagree with the following:

a. Professional educators should always consult with parents before instituting major changes in school curriculum.

_____ Strongly agree   _____ Agree   _____ Disagree   _____ Strongly disagree

b. Professional educators should always consult with parents before making major curricular changes in the area of Family Life/Sex Education.

_____ Strongly agree   _____ Agree   _____ Disagree   _____ Strongly disagree

c. Professional educators should have the final say in decisions involving curricular matters.

_____ Strongly agree   _____ Agree   _____ Disagree   _____ Strongly disagree

d. Parents should have the final say in decisions involving Family Life/Sex Education in the schools.

_____ Strongly agree   _____ Agree   _____ Disagree   _____ Strongly disagree

e. Professional educators should have the final say in decisions involving school administration.

_____ Strongly agree   _____ Agree   _____ Disagree   _____ Strongly disagree

f. It is the school administration's responsibility to reflect the educational programs desired by parents.

_____ Strongly agree _____ Agree _____ Disagree _____ Strongly disagree

COMMENTS: Please make any comments which you think may be of interest to us about your district's action with regard to Family Life/Sex Education. Since we rely on you as an expert on your district, anything you wish to tell us will be of great importance. We would also find invaluable any literature you have on such activities in your district. Please send such literature to us. Thank you.

Section A

This section may be filled out by a clerk, a secretary, or by the superintendent.

A1. Does your district include a local governmental unit (e.g. a city or a village) which has a population of 10,000 or more?

_____ No (go to Q.A2) _____ Yes

IF YES: Ala. Name of governmental unit (e.g., Grinnell, Iowa)
_____

Alb. About what percentage of your students reside within that unit? _____ %

A2. What is the starting salary in your district for a teacher with a Bachelor's degree and no teaching experience? $ _____ /year

A3. How many teachers does your district employ? (Do not include teacher's aides.)

_____ Full time
_____ Part time

A4. How many non-teaching professionals (e.g. psychologists, administrators, social workers, etc. *not* including clerks) does your district employ?

_____ Full time
_____ Part time

A5. Does your district employ a business manager?

_____ Yes, full time _____ No
_____ Yes, part time

A6a. What is your current operating budget? (Please be exact.)

$\rule{3cm}{0.4pt}$

A6b. What proportion of your budget is raised with local taxes?

_____ Percent

A7. Does your district employ an audio-visual aids director?

_____ Yes, full time   _____ No
_____ Yes, part time

A8. Does your district employ a personnel director?

_____ Yes, full time   _____ No
_____ Yes, part time

A9. Does your district have a curriculum director or a comparable position?

_____ Yes, full time   _____ No
_____ Yes, part time

A10. How many employees of your district are involved *solely* in curriculum planning, development, review, or revision?

_____ None
_____ # Professional
_____ # Nonprofessional

A11. Was a referendum on Family Life/Sex Education ever held in your district?

_____ Yes   _____ No (If no, go to Q.A13)

A12. IF YES: Please list the years and the results of such a referendum (If numbers are not available, did it pass or fail?)

YEAR	# VOTES FOR	# VOTES AGAINST

A13. Was an opinion poll of public sentiment on Family Life/Sex Education ever taken in your district?

_____ No   _____ Yes (please list the years and the results)

YEAR	FOR	% AGAINST	% UNDECIDED

A14. Did your district hold a referendum after 1960 on the subject of issuing school bonds?

_____ Yes   _____ No

A15. IF YES: Using the following space, please fill in the years such referenda were held, what the bonds were for, and the votes for and against the issue. (If the figures are unavailable, would you please tell us whether it passed or failed.)

YEAR   BONDS WERE FOR ...   VOTES IN FAVOR   VOTES AGAINST

Section B

This section may be filled out either by a specialist in Family Life/Sex Education courses, a curriculum director, or by the school superintendent.

B1. Does your district have or has it had a planned program of Family Life/Sex Education?

_____ Currently has a planned program of Family Life/Sex Education (Answer Q.2+3)

_____ Once had a planned program of Family Life/Sex Education (Answer Q.4+5)

_____ Does not have and has not had a planned program of Family Life/Sex Education (Go to Q.6)

IF THE PROGRAM IS CURRENTLY IN OPERATION:

B2. How many of your district's professional staff are involved solely in this program? _____

B3. What is the approximate number of different books and audio-visual materials employed in the program?

number of books _____
number of audio-visual materials _____
(Go to Q.6)

IF YOU HAD BUT DO NOT CURRENTLY HAVE A PROGRAM:

B4. How many of your district's professional staff were involved solely in this program? _____

B5. What was the approximate number of different books and audio-visual materials employed in the program?

number of books _____
number of audio-visual materials _____

B6. We are interested in finding out some things about the curriculum in your district. Listed on the following page are a number of topics. They are not necessarily all found in the same curriculum. There are six columns following each topic. Please enter the appropriate information in each column. If a topic has never been included in your curriculum, leave the spaces for it blank and go on to the next topic.

Topics	Lowest grade taught	Year subject initially taught	Is it in a planned Family Life Sex Education course? Yes or No	Is it 1) elective 2) required 3) excused*	Taught			If eliminated, Year eliminated
					coed	only boys	only girls	
Anatomy of Generative Organs		19___						19___
Animal Reproduction		19___						19___
Human Reproduction		19___						19___
Menstrual Hygiene		19___						19___
Seminal Emissions		19___						19___
Masturbation		19___						19___
Prostitution		19___						19___
Venereal Diseases		19___						19___
Physical, Emotional, and Social Changes in Adolescence		19___						19___
Dating, Petting, Necking		19___						19___
Planned Parenthood		19___						19___
Peer Relationships (Including Boy-Girl)		19___						19___
Development of Ethical Standards		19___						19___
Other (specify)		19___						19___

*This is a required course from which a student may be excused during the teaching of the topic.

Notes

Introduction

1. Mary Breasted, *Oh! Sex Education* (New York: Praeger, 1970).
2. Robert Dahl, *Preface to Democratic Theory* (Chicago: University of Chicago, 1956).
3. A thought-provoking study is Robert Crain, Elihu Katz, and Donald Rosenthal's *Politics of Community Conflict* (Indianapolis: Bobbs Merril, 1969).
4. Breasted, p. 312.

Chapter 1
The Politico-Moral Principles of
Sex Education in the Schools

1. Richard Flacks, *Youth and Social Change* (Chicago: Markham, 1971), p. 22.
2. Ibid., pp. 22-25. Works discussing the historical importance of public policies involving issues of self-indulgence and self-restraint are Gusfield, *Symbolic Crusaders* (Urbana: University of Illinois Press, 1963) especially pp. 4, 29-31, 142; on right-wing politics, see S.M. Lipset and E. Raab, *The Politics of Unreason* (New York: Harper and Row, 1970) pp. 117-19: the movement for juvenile courts is briefly discussed in these terms by Anthony M. Platt, *The Childsavers: the Invention of Delinquency* (Chicago: University of Chicago Press, 1969), especially p. 144. Although Robert S. Pickett does not view the juvenile court in the way Platt does, he does present evidence that family authority and self-indulgence were crucial impetuses for changes in the juvenile penal system. See his *House of Refuge: Origins of Juvenile Reform in New York: 1815-1857* (Syracuse: University of Syracuse Press, 1967). For a discussion of attitude toward drugs in these terms, see Troy Duster, *The Legislation of Morality: Law, Drugs, and Moral Judgment* (New York: Free Press, 1970). See also Leon R. Kass, "Making Babies-the New Biology and the 'Old' Morality," *Public Interest*, no. 26 (Winter 1972), pp. 18-56.
3. Joseph Gusfield, *Symbolic Crusaders*, p. 187; also Richard Hofstadter, *Anti-Intellectualism in American Life* (New York: Knopf, 1969), p. 133.
4. James S. Coleman, *Community Conflict* (New York: Free Press & McMillan, 1957) p. 4. Another prerequisite to conflict is that community members must feel that action can be taken. See also Martin Shapiro, *Freedom of Speech: The Supreme Court and Judicial Review* (Englewood Cliffs, N.J.: Prentice Hall, 1966), p. 136.
5. Esther D. Schulz and Sally R. Williams, *Family Life and Sex Education:*

Curriculum and Instruction (New York: Harcourt, Brace, and World, 1968), p. 4.

6. Sex Information and Education Council of the United States, *Sexuality and Man* (New York: Scribners, 1970), p. 140.

7. Compare Mary Breasted, *Oh! Sex Education* (New York: Praeger, 1970), pp. 329-30; E. Van Den Haag, "Why Sex Education?" *National Review* 21 (23 September 1969): 956-58: Russel Kirk, "Schools and Moral Instruction: California and Michigan," *National Review* 21 (29 July 1969): 752. Sources of literature of the so-called radical right reflecting this theme are Gordon Drake, "Do the Schools Have the Proper Place to Teach Raw Sex" (Tulsa: Christian Crusade, 1969); Gordon Drake, *SIECUS: Corrupter of Youth* (Tulsa: Christian Crusade, 1969); Phoebe Courtney, *The Sex Education Racket* (New Orleans: Free Men Speak, Inc., 1969); Movement to Restore Democracy (MOTOREDE), "Sex Education in the Schools: Some Thoughts from Eminent Doctors and from MOTOREDE." Those on the President's Obscenity Commission who voted in favor of the majority position that advocates elimination of many antipornography laws and would rely heavily on school sex education to reduce interest in pornography gloss over both some of the empirical bases, but more importantly over the degree their own moral position affects the findings. See James Q. Wilson "Violence, Pornography, and Social Sciences," *Public Interest* no. 22 (Winter 1971), pp. 45-61. In his report, Commissioner Joseph Clapper comes closest to giving an accurate picture of the relationship between those commissioners' values and their policy recommendations: "The right of adults to read and say what they please is so precious a freedom that I would wish to protect it from any encroachment not dictated by clear, *unambiguous evidence* of social danger" (Report of the President's Commission on Obscenity and Pornography [New York: Bantam, 1970], p. 444, our emphasis.) For more on this relationship between morality and policy evaluation when impact of a policy is uncertain, see Duster, pp. 29-54. For a more general but informative discussion, see William E. Connally, *Political Science and Ideology* (New York: Atherton, 1967).

8. See the statements by dissenting commissioners in *The Report on Obscenity and Pornography*, p. 456. ff.

9. Ibid., p. 458.

10. These are from the statements by commissioners dissenting from the majority report of the *Report of the Commission on Obscenity and Pornography*, pp. 458, 500. We shall subsequently say more about this report, in which the conflict over school sex education plays a major role.

11. Anne Small Miller, "Personal Hygiene for Teen-agers," *Volta Review*, April 1964, p. 64.

12. Quoted in *Sexuality and Man*, p. vii.

13. *Report on Obscenity and Pornography*, p. 53.

14. See Breasted, pp. 280-326 for an excellent description of this.

15. See Gertrude J. Selznick and Stephen Steinberg, *The Tenacity of Prejudice: Anti-Semitism in Contemporary America* (New York: Harper and Row, 1967), p. 157.

16. "Massachusetts Board of Education, First Annual Report," in Robert K. Bremer (ed.), *Children and Youth in America: A Documentary History*, vol. 2, (Cambridge, Mass.: Harvard University Press, 1970), p. 1448. See generally 1447-51.

17. See, for example, Esther D. Schulz and Sally R. Williams.

18. *Sexuality and Man* (New York: Scribners, 1970), p. 157.

19. Mary Breasted, pp. 128-29.

20. *Sexuality and Man*, p. 155. See also p. 136.

21. *Report on Obscenity and Pornography*, p. 169.

22. Wilson; Murray Kempton, "The Feelthy Commission," *New York Review of Books* 15 (Nov. 19, 1970): 24-25. In fact, rigorous empirical standards are seldom used by proponents to evaluate the success of the sex education programs. The President's Obscenity Commission made a small but inconclusive attempt at measuring impact. Other proponents pay disconcertingly little attention to the questions of evaluation of their program. They often state their goals in terms that at one extreme are extremely vague but important or at the other extreme are specific but banal. See, for instance, Helen Manley, *Family Life and Sex Education in the Elementary School* (Washington, D.C.: Elementary, Kindergarten and Nursery Education Association of the United States, 1968), pp. 19-20, who argues that "the more immediate results of a good program" must be the disappearance of graffiti, the elimination of snickering over pornography, and the telling of sex-related jokes. Other immediate effects include an increase in openness and respect toward the opposite sex.

23. Edmond Cahn, "Jurisprudence," *New York University Law Review* 30 (1955): 167. Reprinted by permission.

24. Gusfield, *Symbolic Crusaders*, p. 180.

25. *The Report of the Commission on Obscenity and Pornography* (New York: Bantam, 1970), p. 317.

Chapter 2
Sex Education: The Orientation Issue

1. Harold M. Proshansky and Richard I. Evans, "The Radical Right: A Threat to the Behavioral Sciences," *Journal of Social Issues* 19 (January 1963): 86-106.

2. Alfred Auerbach, "The Anti-Sex Movement: The Attack on Sex Education." Paper delivered at the 123rd Annual Meeting of the American Psychiatric Association, San Francisco, May 11-15, 1970.

3. Ibid.

4. For a somewhat similar discussion, see Robert Crain, Elihu Katz, and Richard Rosenthal, *Politics of Community Conflict* (Indianapolis: Bobbs-Merrill, 1969), pp. 3-15.

5. Joseph R. Gusfield, *The Symbolic Crusaders: Status Politics and the American Temperance Movement* (Urbana, Ill.: University of Illinois Press, 1963), p. 144.

6. See his "Moral Passage: The Symbolic Process in the Designation of Deviance," *Social Forces* 15 (Fall 1969): 175-88.

7. S.M. Lipset and Earl Raab, *The Politics of Unreason: Right Wing Extremism in America, 1790-1970* (New York: Harper and Row, 1970).

8. The term *status politics* is usually associated with Richard Hofstadter. Though Hofstadter was not always explicit in maintaining this view of cultural fundamentalism, he did display similar views. For example, he views the most rabid anti-Communists of the McCarthy period as not primarily concerned with communism at all. Their hidden but most important aim was "to discharge resentments and frustrations, to punish, to satisfy enmities whose sorts lay elsewhere than in the communist issue itself" (*Anti-Intellectualism in American Life* [New York: Knopf, 1969], p. 41, also p. 114, 130-131). See also his *The Age of Reform* (New York: Knopf, 1955) and "The Pseudo-Conservative Revolt" in Daniel Bell (ed.), *The New American Right* (New York: Criterion Books, 1955), pp. 43-45; see also Lipset and Raab, pp. 114, 117-18, 392. Certainly these explanations are related to the values of status politics theorists, because as Judith Shklar suggests, political analysts have a tendency to identify policy positions they agree with as "real" and call others "symbolic." See Judith Shklar, *Legalism* (Cambridge, Mass.: Harvard University Press, 1964), pp. 92-97. The best general analyses of the social values of some of the status politics theorists is Michael Paul Rogin, *The Intellectuals and McCarthy: The Radical Spectre* (Cambridge, Mass.: MIT Press, 1967).

9. Murray Edelman, *The Symbolic Uses of Politics* (Urbana, Ill.: University of Illinois, 1967), p. 164.

10. Murray Edelman, "Myths, Metaphors, and Political Conformity," *Psychiatry* 30 (1967): 217-28; *The Symbolic Uses of Politics*, p. 154-56, 158. A relevant discussion of the ways in which the symbolic emphasis of the psychological approach inaccurately minimizes the appeal radical-right views have for the average men is found in Crain, et al., pp. 52-72.

11. Edelman, *The Symbolic Uses of Politics*, pp. 152-71.

12. In this light, James Coleman mistakenly suggests that only one side derives its strength from its ability to so derogate the opposition. With this limitation, his statement below is a good description of the relationship between political tactics and social values. "In certain circumstances one side [in a community conflict] derives much of its strength from personal attack and derogation, that is, from techniques which, were they not legitimated by patriotism or sex codes or similar strong values, would be outlawed in a

community. Thus the degree that such methods are permitted, the attackers gain, and the degree that community norms are upheld against these methods, the advantage is to the attacked. The more the attacked side can invoke norms defining legitimate controversy, the more likely it is to win" (James S. Coleman, *Community Conflict* [New York: Free Press, MacMillan, 1957], p. 12).

13. The question of the effect of defining a political issue as a moral one has received little attention from social scientists. Those who touch upon the subject suggest that the perception of an issue as a moral one increases the degree of social control that can be used against the opposition. An example is Wirt's interpretation of President Lyndon Johnson's civil rights activities:

Thus he [LBJ] was the first President to present the American people squarely with what lay at the heart of the whole struggle when in his nationwide address . . . he put it simply: "We are confronted primarily with a moral issue." It was not a political issue, as Southerners had said for so long, seeking to cast segregation in a bin along with a battleship contract, a road route, and a postmaster appointment in Round Bottom, Ohio. (Frederick M. Wirt, *Politics of Southern Equality: Law and Social Change in a Mississippi County* [Chicago: Aldine, 1970], p. 181.)

Similarly, Clive Barnes in his introduction to *The Report of the Commission on Obscenity and Pornography* says:

The easiest thing to censor—or if you prefer it, to suppress—is something of a sexual nature. You merely have to say that it offends you morally, and in breathless, bible-tapping guilt, a considerable part of the community is likely to support you.

14. See the text accompanying note 24 in chapter one.

15. Gusfield, pp. 177-86.

16. Gertrude J. Selznick and Stephen Steinberg, *The Tenacity of Prejudice: Anti Semitism in Contemporary America* (New York: Harper and Row, 1969), chapter 8.

17. For the best overall discussion, see Frederick Wirt and Michael Kirst, *The Political Web of American Schools* (Boston: Little, Brown, 1972).

18. These two greatly accepted definitions of politics are developed in Harold Lasswell, *Politics: Who Gets What, When, How* (Cleveland: Meridan, 1958), and David Easton, *The Political System* (New York: Knopf, 1971), respectively.

19. Robert Agger and Marshall Goldstein, *Who Will Rule the Schools: A Cultural Class Crisis* (Belmont, Calif.: Wadsworth, 1971).

Chapter 3
Community Educational Policy Making

1. We use the term "schoolman" generically though in fact there are almost no women school superintendents.

2. Everett M. Rogers, *The Diffusion of Innovation* (New York: The Free Press, 1962).

3. Robert Crain, Elihu Katz and Donald Rosenthal, *The Politics of Community Conflict* (Indianapolis: Bobbs Merrill, 1969).

4. Dale Mann, "Public Relations as Community Control in Urban Education," paper presented to American Political Association, Washington, D.C., September 1972. See also Robert Agger and Marshall Goldstein, *Who Will Rule the Schools: A Cultural Class Crisis* (Belmont, Calif.: Wadsworth, 1972), p. 191.

5. Neal Gross, Ward S. Mason and Alexander McEachern, *Explorations in Role Analysis: Studies of the School Superintendency Role* (New York: John Wiley & Sons, 1968).

6. Mann.

7. Rogers, p. 243.

8. Richard O. Carlson, *Adoption of Educational Innovations* (Eugene, Ore.: Center for the Advanced Study of Educational Administration, 1965).

9. See, for instance, Kenneth Dolbeare and Phillip Hammond, *The School Prayer Decision* (Chicago: University of Chicago Press, 1971).

10. F.W. Wirt and Michael Kirst, *The Political Web of American Schools* (Boston: Little, Brown, 1972), p. 85.

11. Ibid., pp. 208-211; 223-226.

12. Ibid.

13. Agger and Goldstein.

14. Ibid., p. 26.

15. Dolbeare and Hammond.

16. Agger and Goldstein, pp. 23-26.

17. James S. Coleman, *Community Conflict* (New York: Free Press, 1957); Louis Masotti, *Education and Politics in Suburbia* (Cleveland: Western Reserve University, 1967).

18. William Gamson, "Rancorous Conflict in Community Politics," *American Sociological Review* 31 (1966): 71-81.

19. Coleman.

20. Dolbeare and Hammond, pp. 109-110.

21. Agger and Goldstein, p. 164.

22. Mann.

23. Dolbeare and Hammond, pp. 7-8, 106.

24. For a discussion of the policy process that stresses elite discretion, see Murray Edelman, *Politics as Symbolic Action* (Chicago: Markham, 1971).

25. William Gamson, *Power and Discontent* (Homewood, Ill.: Dorsey, 1968), p. 32. Our discussion is generally based on pp. 21-32.

26. Ibid., p. 112.

27. Ibid., p. 135; Phillip Selznick, *TVA and the Grass Roots* (Berkeley: University of California, 1953).

28. Dolbeare and Hammond, p. 108.

29. J. Victor Baldridge, *Power and Conflict in the University* (New York: Wiley, 1971).

Chapter 4
Professionalization and Innovation

1. Advisory Committee on Social Hygiene Education, New Jersey Department of Education, "An Approach in Schools to Education for Personal and Family Living," *Journal of Social Hygiene* 38 (February 1952): 57.

2. "Parents Get Blame for Lack of Sex Education Programs," *Nation's Schools* 77 (May 1966): 95.

3. "Schoolmen Disagree with Critics of Sex Education," *Nation's Schools* 84 (July 1969): 47.

4. Joanne Zazzaro, "Americans Do Support Sex Education," *American School Board Journal* 157 (September 1969): 32.

5. Reuben H. Benlmer, "Family Life Education Survey," *Marriage and Family Living* 23 (1961): 299-301.

6. Lee G. Burchinal, "Sources and Adequacy of Sex Knowledge Among Iowa School Girls," *Marriage and Family Living* 22 (1969): 258-69.

7. "NEA News" (Washington, D.C.: National Educational Association: Press, Radio, and Television Relations, 27 May 1969).

8. See Robert Crain, Elihu Katz, and Donald Rosenthal, *Politics of Community Conflict*, (Indianapolis: Bobbs Merrill, 1969), pp. 52-72.

9. This appears in an article by Lester Kirkendall and Helen Cox in July-August 1967 *Children*, quoted and discussed in Mary Breasted, *Oh! Sex Education* (New York: Praeger, 1969), pp. 139-40.

10. Beatrice M. Gudridge, *Sex Education in Schools* (Washington: National School Public Relations Association, 1969), p. 32.

11. Ibid., p. 4.

12. We also asked the superintendents: how many professional associations they belonged to; how many journals they normally read; and how many professional meetings they had attended in the twelve months prior to filling out the questionnaires. The answers to these questions were intended to provide direct measures of cosmopolitanism. However, the questions proved unreliable because of the judgmental and perhaps overly general quality of the information requested. Therefore, these measures of cosmopolitanism are not used.

13. Measuring the timing of innovation is important but difficult. We have been forced to rely on recall information. The reliability of recall information is often questionable. For a thoughtful discussion of the importance and difficulties of measuring time of innovation, see Elihu Katz, Martin L. Levin and Herbert Hamilton, "Traditions of Research on the Diffusion of Innovation," *American Sociological Review* 28 (1963), especially pp. 241-43.

Chapter 5
Sex Education Policy Making and
The Failure of The Opposition

1. Robert Crain, Elihu Katz and Richard Rosenthal, *The Politics of Community Conflict* (Indianapolis: Bobbs-Merrill, 1969), pp. 92-93.
2. Compare Kenneth Dolbeare and Phillip Hammond, *The School Prayer Decision* (Chicago: University of Chicago Press, 1971).

Chapter 6
Innovativeness Reconsidered

1. Robert Alford, *Bureaucracy and Participation*, (Chicago: Rand McNally, 1969), pp. 2-3.
2. Crain, Katz and Rosenthal emphasize the strength of this predisposition to mobilize. In general, communities that adopted fluoridation were those with governments that were most centralized and most insulated from the masses. But mobilizable communities also had more success than any other type of community in gaining the fluoridation adoption by referendum, the *least* centralized form of policy making. They attribute this referendum success to the fact that these communities mobilized so quickly to consider fluoridation, that they adopted it before the issue became nationally controversial.
3. Ibid., chapter 10; Robert Crain, Elihu Katz and Donald B. Rosenthal, *Politics of Community Conflict* (Indianapolis: Bobbs Merrill, 1969), pp. 166-67.
4. Alford, p. 184.
5. Ibid., p. 31.
6. Gideon Sjoberg, Richard Bryner, and Buford Harris, "Bureaucracy and the Lower Class," *Sociology and Social Research* 50 (1966): 325-36.
7. See Alford's discussion of schools, pp. 54, 71-72, 92-95, 109-111; Frederick Wirt and Michael Kirst briefly discuss the tensions between bureaucracy and participation as applied to schools in the *Political Web of American Schools* (Boston: Little, Brown, 1972), p. 95.
8. Mobilization of bias is a term coined by E.E. Schattschneider in *The Semi-Sovereign People* (New York: Holt, Rinehart, and Winston, 1960), p. 20.

Chapter 7
Sex Education in Anaheim and Statetown:
Two Case Studies

1. Mary Breasted, *Oh! Sex Education* (New York: Frederick Praeger, 1970).
2. Diana and Neil Onerhiem provided invaluable and dedicated assistance in collecting the Statetown data.

3. Ibid., p. 128.

4. Ibid., p. 157-58.

5. William K. Muir, Jr., *Defending "The Hill Against Metal Houses*, ICP Case Series, no. 26 (University, Ala.: University of Alabama Press, revised, 1960).

6. Breasted, pp. 35-36.

7. Ibid.

8. For a study of community conflict focusing in community disintegration as a cause of issue conflict, see Louis H. Masotti, *Education and Politics in Suburbia* (Cleveland: Western Reserve University Press, 1967).

Chapter 8
Sex Education and Social Control:
Some Broader Issues in the Politics
of Education

1. William A. Gamson, *Power and Discontent*, (Homewood, Ill.: Dorsey, 1968), pp. 193-94.

2. For a relevant discussion of the uses of social theory, see Robert S. Cahill, "Notes on the Uses of Political Theory: The Case of Theory as a Guide to Practical Action," paper presented at 1972 annual meeting of the American Political Science Association, Washington, D.C., September 5-9, 1972.

3. Partisans may also pay little attention to policy implementation because they are primarily concerned simply with having government grant legitimacy to their position. See Joseph Gusfield, *Symbolic Crusaders* (Urbana, Ill.: University of Illinois, 1963), p. 121.

4. *Valent v. N.J. Board of Education*, 274 A.2d. 832, 114 N.J. Super. 63 (197).

5. *Cornwell v. Md.*, 314 F. Supp. 340, 341 (D.C.Md. 1969).

6. *Hopkins v. Hamden Bd. of Education*, 289 A. 2d. 914, 923 (N.J. Court of Common Pleas 1971).

7. *Hopkins v. Hamden Bd. of Education*, 289 A.2d. 914 (1971); *Cornwell v. Maryland*, 314 F. Supp. 340 (D.C.Md. 1969). In the latter case the SEP opponents cited no authorities for their contention; in the *Hopkins* case, Catholic Church authorities were cited. In a case involving a district attorney's threat to close down a Unitarian Church's sex education program because it allegedly violated a state obscenity statute, a federal district court judge stressed the family's role in sex education. He defended the program on the grounds that families still had the primary role in teaching sex education and that the parents may have at their disposal facilities for sex education that present these ideas in a religious and ethical framework that the public schools lack. He did not argue, however, that parents have sole authority. *Unitarian Church West v. McConnell*, 337 F. Supp. 1252 (D.D.Wis. 1972).

8. *Valent v. N.J. Bd. of Education*, 288 A.2d. 52 (1972).

9. *Valent v. N.J. Bd. of Education*, 274 A.2d. 832, 840 (1971).

10. Note, "The Constitutionality under the Religious Clauses of The First Amendment of Compulsory Sex Education in Public Schools," *Michigan Law Review* 68 (April 1972): 1050-61.

11. Much of the following argument is based on note, "The Constitutionality under the Religious Clauses of the First Amendment of Compulsory Sex Education in Public Schools."

12. John Rawls, *A Theory of Justice* (Cambridge: Harvard, 1971), p. 219. Our discussion in this paragraph is informed by Rawls's discussion of "Toleration of the Intolerant" (Ibid., pp. 216-221).

13. Gamson, p. 8.

14. Angus Campbell, et al., *The American Voter* (New York: John Wiley & Sons, 1960).

15. For an interesting empirical study of changing authority patterns and the implications of these changes for participation in policy making, see Michael Otten, *University Authority and the Student* (Berkeley: University of California Press, 1970).

Appendix A
The Data

1. Robert L. Crain, Elihu Katz, and Donald B. Rosenthal, *The Politics of Community Conflict* (New York: Bobbs-Merrill, 1969).

2. The source of the mailing list was, National Center for Educational Statistics, *Education Directory: Public School Systems*, 1968-69/part 2 (Washington: U.S. Office of Education, 1969).

3. "Parents Get Blame for Lack of Sex Education Programs," *Nation's Schools* 77 (May 1966): p. 95. "Schoolmen Disagree with Critics of Sex Education," *Nation's Schools* 84 (July 1969): p. 47.

Index

Agger, Robert, 26, 27
Alford, Robert, 65
American Medical Association (A.M.A.),
    xvii
Anaheim, California, xvii, 73 ff.
Authority
  definition of, 100
  and participation
    conflict between, 26
    issue, 101
  of schoolmen, 32

Behavioral science, 13
Breasted, Mary, xvii, xx, 9, 73 ff.
Bureaucratic methods of conflict resolution,
    90
Bureaucratization
  of conflict, 32, 51
  and innovation, 64-66

Cahn, Edmond, 9
Calderone, Mary, xvii
Carlson, Richard O., 25
Christian Crusade, xvii
Cognitive vs. psychological explanation, 17
Commission on Obscenity and Pornography,
    xvii, 5, 8, 9, 11
Comprehensiveness of sex education pro-
    grams, 57
Conflict
  in Anaheim and Statetown, 87 ff.
  authority vs. political participation, 26
  bureaucratization of, 32, 51
  causes of rancorous, 27
  culture-class, 26
  and innovation, tension between, 21, 30
  management mechanisms, 52
  minimization of, 30
    strategies, 52 ff.
  politico-moral, 14
  resolution, bureaucratic methods of, 90
Consideration of sex education
  and innovativeness, 44, 45
  and professionalization, 42-44
  and speed of innovation, 45, 46
Consumption-oriented society, 1
Content-alteration strategies, 33
Control
  ethic, 3, 6
  schools as agents of, 6, 97, 100
Co-optation and bureaucracy participation
    conflict, 66
Co-optative
  mechanisms

and opposition, 57 ff.
  and program content, 57 ff.
  strategies, 31
Cosmopolitanism, 43
Counterinfluence, 49, 52, 69, 102
  effectiveness of strategies, 57
  and opposition, 55 ff.
  strategies, 29 ff.
  strategies and opposition, 51 ff.
Crain, Robert L., 23, 48, 49
Culture-class conflict, 26

Dahl, Robert, xix
Denial ethic, 1, 3, 4
Derogation of opponents, 10, 16
Deviance, political, 14 ff.
Diffusion of innovations, 21 ff.
Discontent, management of, 28 ff., 52, 56,
    57
Dolbeare, Kenneth, 27, 28, 31

Edelman, Murray, 15
Efficacy, political, 100

Fanaticicism, 10, 13, 14
Fluoridation, 24, 29, 34, 48, 49, 60, 61
Fundamentalism, moral, 75
Fundamentalist, cultural, 14, 15

Gamson, William, 27, 28, 93
Goldstein, Marshall, 26, 27
Gross, Neal, 24
Gusfield, Joseph, 14, 15, 16

Hammond, Phillip, 27, 28, 31

Innovation
  and bureaucratization, 64-66
  and conflict, tension between, 21 ff.
  diffusion of, 21 ff.
  index, 45
  need for, 32
  normative regulation of, 22
  and participation, xix
  and professionalization, 32
  situational field of, 22
  speed of, 45
Innovativeness
  and consideration of sex education, 44, 45
  of school districts, 63
Issue, definition of, 21

135

136

John Birch Society, xvii, 76

Katz, Elihu, 23, 48, 49

Lipset, Seymour Martin, 15

McEachern, Alexander, 24
Majority, tyrannical, xix
Management of discontent, 28 ff., 56
Mann, Dale, 24, 27, 28
Mann, Horace, 6
Mason, Ward S., 24
Minority, intense, xix
Moral
 conflict in Anaheim, 75
 fundamentalism, 75
 relativism, 3
 traditionalists, 14 ff.
Morality of consequences, 8, 75
 public support for, 11
Muir, William K., 76

National Education Association (N.E.A.),
 xvii, 39
National School Public Relations Association, 40
Normative regulation of innovation, 22

Opponents
 derogation of, 10, 16
 of sex education, 41, 42
Opposition
 and counterinfluence, 55 ff.
 and counterinfluence strategies, 51 ff.
 and participation, 54 ff.
 and program content, 49
 scale, 47

Parents participation in decision-making
 superintendents' attitude towards, 52
Participation
 and authority
  conflict between, 26
  issue, 101
 of citizens in policy-making, 29, 30, 33,
  57
 and innovation, xix
 levels of and conflict minimization strategies, 52 ff.
 and opposition, 54 ff.
 of parents in decision-making
  superintendents' attitude towards, 52
 and professionalization, xix
Pluralism, 3
Political
 conflict approach, 18 ff.

deviance, 14 ff.
efficacy, 100
participation and authority, conflict between, 26
Politico-moral conflict, 14
Politics and psychopathology, 13, 14, 16,
 17
Potential partisans, 28
President's Commission on Obscenity and
 Pornography, xvii, 5, 8, 9, 11
Profession, definition of, 22, 23
Professional publications, support of sex
 education, 38 ff.
Professionalization, 35, 42
 and consideration of sex education, 42-49
 of education administration, 22, 26
 and innovation, 32
 and participation, xix
 of school superintendents, 42-44
Program comprehensiveness, 57
Proponents of sex education, 13, 41, 42
Protestant ethic, 1, 2
Psychopathology and politics, 13, 14, 16,
 17
Public relations model, 24, 25, 27, 46, 77,
 94
 applied to Anaheim and Statetown, 87 ff.

Raab, Earl, 15
Radical right, 13, 27
Rawls, John, 99
Rogers, Everett M., 22, 25
Rosenthal, Donald B., 23, 48, 49

School superintendents, 21
 and consideration of sex education, 42-44
 professionalization of, 42-44
Sex education
 comprehensiveness of programs, 47, 50
 opponents of, 41, 42
 proponents of, 41, 42
Sex Information and Education Council of
 the United States (S.I.E.C.U.S.), xvii,
 4, 74
Situational field of innovation, 22
Social control, 6, 97-100
Strategies, content alteration, 33
Status politics, 15 ff.
 as explanation of Anaheim controversy,
  74 ff.

Traditionalist, moral, xix, 14 ff.

Value-conflict theory, 14
Value relativism, 3

Wirt, Frederick, 28

About the Authors

James Hottois is Assistant Professor of Political Science and Assistant Dean of the College of Arts and Sciences, University of San Diego. He has taught at Grinnell College and holds the Ph.D. in Political Science from the State University of New York at Buffalo.

Neal A. Milner is Associate Professor of Political Science at the University of Hawaii. He has taught at Grinnell College and Northwestern University, and holds the Ph.D. in Political Science from the University of Wisconsin. Professor Milner is the author of *Courts and Local Law Enforcement: The Impact of Miranda* (Beverly Hills: Sage Publications, 1971), and he is coeditor of *Black Politics: The Inevitability of Conflict* (New York: Holt, Rinehart, and Winston, 1971).